ADIRONDACKS

TRAVEL GUIDE

2025

Discover Adirondacks's Accommodations, tourist attractions and spots. Practical Tips and Local Insights

Julienne Lemelin

Table of Contents

INTRODUCTION

History & Customs

The Adirondacks are a place that seems to breathe with a life of
its own, a region where history and customs weave together
seamlessly with the land itself. It's hard to talk about the
Adirondacks without feeling a certain sense of reverence, as if
every rock, tree, and stream has a story to tell. The moment you
set foot in the area, you can almost feel the weight of its past
mingling with the traditions that its people hold close to their
hearts.

For me, learning about the Adirondacks began not through
textbooks but through conversations and quiet observations
during my visits. It's in the voices of the locals and the way they
carry the knowledge of their forebears that you truly get a sense
of the history. The Adirondacks have been inhabited for
centuries, starting with the Native American tribes who first
called this rugged terrain home. They named the region, and
their connection to the land is palpable in the stories passed
down. Their customs revolved around the seasons, deeply tied
to the rhythms of the mountains and forests. Hunting, fishing,
and foraging were not merely survival skills but acts of
harmony with the environment.

As you walk through the trails or paddle across the pristine
lakes, you might find yourself wondering what it was like when
the first European settlers arrived. These settlers brought their
own traditions, melding them with what they learned from the
Native Americans. This fusion created a unique way of life that
still echoes in the customs of the Adirondacks today. It was a
hard life back then, one defined by long winters, unforgiving
terrain, and a reliance on community. That sense of resilience

and interdependence, though born out of necessity, has become an intrinsic part of the Adirondack spirit.

When you visit a place like Lake Placid, you can almost hear the echoes of the 1932 and 1980 Winter Olympics. The pride the region holds for hosting these events is more than just a nod to sporting history. It's a reflection of how the people here embrace challenge and celebrate achievement. There's a deep respect for physical endurance and the outdoors, something you notice in how locals encourage hiking, skiing, and climbing as ways of life rather than mere activities.

I remember sitting in a rustic lodge one evening, listening to a storyteller recount the logging days of the Adirondacks. Logging was once the lifeblood of the region, but it came at a great cost to the natural environment. Conservation efforts eventually arose, thanks to passionate individuals who recognized the need to protect the area's beauty for future generations. The Adirondack Park, established in the late 19th century, stands as a testament to those efforts. It's one of the first places in the United States where land was set aside as "forever wild." That phrase, forever wild, is spoken with a kind of quiet pride around here, and you can see it reflected in the customs of sustainable living and a deep respect for nature that persist.

One of the most charming things about the Adirondacks is how its traditions are not just preserved but celebrated. Take, for example, the region's love of the arts. Adirondack chairs, those iconic slatted wooden seats, originated here and are a perfect symbol of the region's ethos: simplicity, utility, and a touch of rugged elegance. Craftsmanship is still alive in the area, from intricate basket weaving to the creation of durable canoes. Every piece tells a story, often passed down through generations.

Festivals and gatherings are another cornerstone of Adirondack life. Seasonal fairs bring people together to share food, music, and stories. Maple syrup festivals in the spring, for instance, are a delightful tradition that ties the community to the land. Watching syrup being made, from tapping the trees to boiling the sap, feels like witnessing a ritual that's both ancient and enduring. And the taste! It's like capturing the very essence of the Adirondack forests in a spoonful of liquid gold.

Then there are the customs tied to the outdoors. Hunting and fishing are not just pastimes but ways of connecting to the land, practiced with a respect that feels almost sacred. Even if you're not a hunter or angler yourself, you'll notice how these activities are integrated into the fabric of the community. They're about more than the act itself; they're about teaching patience, honoring the cycles of nature, and fostering a sense of gratitude.

And of course, there's the food. Adirondack cuisine is hearty and unpretentious, the kind of food that nourishes both body and soul. I'll never forget the first time I had a bowl of venison stew at a small mountain inn. It was simple, sure, but it tasted like love and tradition, like someone had taken all the best parts of the region's history and simmered them together. Locally sourced ingredients, like trout fresh from the streams or blueberries picked from the hillsides, make every meal feel like a celebration of the land.

Perhaps what strikes me most about the Adirondacks is the storytelling. Everyone here has a story, and they're often eager to share it. You'll hear about legendary guides who could navigate the wilderness blindfolded or tales of loggers who faced danger with a mix of grit and good humor. Some of the best stories I've heard weren't told in words but in the way someone showed me how to tie a fly for fishing or pointed out the best spot to see the stars.

That brings me to another tradition that feels uniquely Adirondack: stargazing. In a place with so little light pollution, the night sky becomes a breathtaking tapestry. Sitting by a campfire, staring up at a sky so full of stars it almost looks crowded, you can't help but feel connected to something much bigger than yourself. It's moments like these that make you understand why people who live here are so deeply protective of their home.

The customs of the Adirondacks are not just relics of the past; they're living, breathing parts of everyday life. Whether it's the way people greet you with genuine warmth or how they quietly maintain trails and campsites for others to enjoy, there's a sense of stewardship that permeates everything. It's a reminder that history isn't just about what happened before; it's about what we choose to carry forward.

For me, every visit to the Adirondacks feels like a journey through time. It's not just the history written in books or displayed in museums; it's the history you feel in your bones when you're there. It's in the way the mountains seem to hold you, the way the lakes reflect not just the sky but the spirit of everyone who's ever paddled across them. It's a place that leaves you with stories of your own to tell, and a longing to return that never quite fades.

CHAPTER 1: PLANNING YOUR TRIP

Time to visit

The Adirondack region is one of those places that feels magical no matter when you visit. I can tell you, from experience, that this slice of upstate New York offers something unique every season, and it's not just the landscapes but the atmosphere, the people, and even the smells in the air that change so dramatically yet beautifully with the time of year. It's like the Adirondacks have a personality for each season, and each one is worth exploring depending on what you're looking for.

Let's start with the winter, which is when I first fell in love with the Adirondacks. The snow here isn't just snow—it's a blanket that transforms everything into a winter wonderland. I remember arriving after a fresh snowfall, and the world was silent in a way I've never experienced anywhere else. There's a peace that settles over the forests and mountains, as if nature itself is pausing to take a breath. The air is crisp, almost sharp, and you can smell the pines more distinctly than any other time of year. If you love skiing or snowboarding, Whiteface Mountain near Lake Placid is a haven. Even if you're not the sporty type, just sitting by a roaring fire in a cozy lodge, sipping hot cocoa or mulled wine, feels like the most luxurious thing in the world.

Winter in the Adirondacks isn't just about the cold; it's about the coziness it brings. There's something about wrapping yourself in a warm coat, trudging through snowy trails, and then coming back to a snug cabin that makes you appreciate the season more deeply. I've had some of the best conversations over a pot of stew with friends after a day of snowshoeing. You bond over the shared effort of braving the elements, and somehow the stories feel richer and funnier when told in that setting.

Spring in the Adirondacks, though, is an entirely different story. If you've never experienced the smell of the earth waking up, you're missing out. It's as if the entire region takes a deep stretch after a long hibernation. The rivers start to swell with snowmelt, and waterfalls come alive in ways that are almost hypnotic. I once spent hours just sitting by High Falls Gorge, mesmerized by the sheer power of the water rushing past. There's a sense of renewal in the air; the birds come back, the first wildflowers start to poke through the ground, and you can feel the energy of life returning.

One spring, I stayed in a small cabin near Saranac Lake, and every morning, I'd wake up to the sound of loons calling. It's haunting in the best way, a reminder of how connected everything is in this ecosystem. The trails can be a bit muddy in the spring, but honestly, that just adds to the charm. Hiking to Cascade Mountain during this time, I remember the feeling of accomplishment when reaching the summit and looking out over a landscape that was still transitioning from winter to spring. There's something poetic about it—a reminder that change can be messy but beautiful.

Summer, though—that's when the Adirondacks come alive in a way that's almost overwhelming. The lakes, oh the lakes! I don't think I've ever swum in water as clear and refreshing as in Mirror Lake or Lake George. The days are warm but never stifling, and the nights cool down just enough to make sitting by a campfire a delight. I've spent countless evenings toasting marshmallows and swapping stories under a sky so full of stars it takes your breath away. Stargazing in the Adirondacks is something I wish everyone could experience at least once. There's no light pollution, so the Milky Way practically leaps out at you.

Boating, kayaking, paddleboarding—it's all there in summer. I've paddled along quiet inlets where the only sounds were my paddle dipping into the water and the occasional fish jumping. It's meditative in a way that's hard to describe. And if you're into hiking, summer is perfect for tackling the High Peaks. I'll never forget the feeling of standing on the summit of Mount Marcy, the highest point in New York, with the whole of the Adirondacks spread out before me. It's humbling and exhilarating at the same time.

Then there's the fall. Oh, fall in the Adirondacks! It's as if the region was made for this season. The colors are so vibrant they almost don't seem real—fiery reds, golden yellows, deep oranges. It's like walking through a painting. I remember driving along the Adirondack Scenic Byway one October, and I had to pull over more times than I can count just to take it all in. Every turn of the road seemed to reveal an even more stunning vista. There's something about the way the sunlight filters through the changing leaves that feels almost magical.

Apple picking, cider tasting, pumpkin patches—fall is full of these charming little activities that make you feel like a kid again. I spent one fall weekend in Ticonderoga, where I not only enjoyed the foliage but also visited Fort Ticonderoga. The history, combined with the backdrop of fall colors, made it an experience I'll never forget. And the food—fall is when the Adirondacks serve up hearty, comforting meals. I still dream about the apple cider donuts I had at a little roadside stand. They were warm, sugary, and paired perfectly with a cup of fresh cider.

No matter the season, the Adirondacks have a way of drawing you in. Each time I visit, I feel like I'm discovering something new about the place—and about myself. It's the kind of destination that leaves a mark on you, a place you carry with you long after you've left. Whether you're seeking adventure, solitude, or just a break from the everyday grind, the Adirondacks have a way of giving you exactly what you need, even if you didn't know you needed it.

Visa and Entry Requirements

Traveling to the Adirondacks is like stepping into a different world—a place where nature's grandeur meets the simplicity of a slower pace. But before you pack your hiking boots or plan your canoe trips through pristine waters, there's one thing to tackle: the question of how to get there. Specifically, the visa and entry requirements you'll need to meet. Trust me, I've been through it, and while it's not overly complicated, knowing the details ahead of time can save you from unnecessary headaches.

Let me start with the basics. If you're a U.S. citizen, you're in luck. The Adirondacks are within New York state, so all you really need is some form of identification to confirm who you are if necessary. I remember my first trip there—I tossed my driver's license in my pocket and didn't think much more about it. However, if you're traveling from outside the United States, it's a little more complex. That's where visas and other entry requirements come into play.

When I hosted a friend from Europe who wanted to join me on an Adirondack adventure, we had to dive into the visa details. For travelers from countries participating in the Visa Waiver Program (VWP), the process is refreshingly straightforward. My friend, for instance, needed an ESTA—an Electronic System for Travel Authorization. Applying for it online took just a few minutes. We filled out the form together one evening, sipping coffee and laughing at how meticulous the questions seemed to be. Make sure you have your passport handy because you'll need those details, along with your travel plans. The approval came through quickly, within 24 hours. If your country isn't part of the VWP, you'll need to apply for a visitor visa, and that's where things can get a little more time-consuming.

I've also had friends from Canada join me in the Adirondacks, and their experience was a breeze. Thanks to the close relationship between the U.S. and Canada, Canadian citizens don't usually need a visa for short visits. A valid passport is enough. That said, it's always a good idea to double-check, especially if you're staying longer or plan to mix work with your travel. One of my friends nearly forgot her passport at home, and we had to turn back mid-drive to retrieve it. Lesson learned—always triple-check your essentials.

For those coming from farther afield, like Asia or South America, the process often involves a little more preparation. A friend of mine from India had to apply for a B-2 visitor visa, which required an appointment at the U.S. consulate. He went through a thorough interview process, proving he had strong ties to his home country and sufficient funds for his trip. I remember him calling me after his interview, excited but relieved it was over. It took about two weeks for his visa to be approved, so if you're in a similar situation, plan ahead.

Another thing to keep in mind is the importance of having a valid passport. It sounds obvious, right? But I've seen people scramble at the last minute because their passport was about to expire. Make sure it's valid for at least six months beyond your planned departure date from the U.S. This is a standard rule for many countries, and the U.S. is no exception. I've even made it a habit to check my passport's expiry date whenever I book a trip, just to avoid any last-minute panic.

Let's talk about traveling with kids, too. If you're bringing your family to experience the Adirondacks, there are extra considerations. I've traveled with friends who had their kids in tow, and while the requirements weren't overwhelming, they did need to carry additional documentation. A child traveling with only one parent or a guardian might need a notarized letter of consent from the absent parent. It's a precaution to prevent unauthorized travel with minors, and while it might seem tedious, it's an important step.

Now, let me share a tip that saved me some time during one of my trips. If you're a frequent traveler or planning to visit other parts of the U.S. beyond the Adirondacks, consider enrolling in a trusted traveler program like Global Entry or NEXUS. I applied for Global Entry after my second Adirondack trip, and it's been a game-changer. Not only does it expedite entry into the U.S., but it also includes TSA PreCheck, which makes airport security a breeze. The application process does take some time—you'll need to complete an online form and attend an in-person interview—but for me, the convenience has been worth every penny.

One thing that's easy to overlook is the customs declaration form you'll fill out upon arrival in the U.S., whether you're flying in or crossing a land border. I've stood in those lines at customs, watching people nervously second-guess their answers. It's simple, really—just be honest about what you're bringing into the country. The Adirondacks are known for their wildlife and natural beauty, so you don't want to risk bringing anything that could harm the local ecosystem. That means no plants, seeds, or food items that might be restricted. I remember once declaring a bag of trail mix I'd brought from home, just to be safe. The customs officer waved me through with a smile, but I was glad I hadn't tried to sneak anything past.

While the entry requirements themselves aren't overly complicated, the key to a smooth experience is preparation. I always tell people to start early. Check the specific requirements for your nationality, gather your documents, and double-check the details. If you're flying, make sure your airline ticket matches the name on your passport exactly. I've seen people get delayed because of a tiny mismatch—like using a nickname instead of their full legal name.

And don't forget about health-related considerations. While vaccinations aren't typically required for entry into the U.S., it's a good idea to stay up to date on routine vaccines. When I visited during the height of the COVID-19 pandemic, there were additional protocols in place, like providing proof of vaccination or a negative test result. These requirements have since eased, but it's always worth checking for any updates, especially if there are global health concerns.

Finally, let's talk about the practicalities of arriving in the Adirondacks themselves. Most international travelers will fly into a major city like New York City or Boston before making their way upstate. From there, you'll likely rent a car or take a regional flight closer to the area. I've found that having a rental car is the best way to explore the Adirondacks, as public transportation options can be limited. Plus, there's something magical about driving through winding mountain roads, with the trees forming a canopy overhead and the promise of adventure just around the corner.

In the end, the process of meeting visa and entry requirements is just a small part of the journey, but it's an essential one. With a bit of planning and preparation, you'll be ready to step into the natural wonderland of the Adirondacks without a hitch. Whether you're hiking up Whiteface Mountain, paddling through Lake Placid, or simply soaking in the tranquility of a quiet forest, it's all worth it. And when you're there, you'll hardly remember the paperwork it took to get you through the door. Trust me, I've been there, and every single step is worth it.

What to pack

When you're planning a trip to the Adirondacks, packing can feel like an adventure in itself. Trust me, I've been there—staring at an empty suitcase, wondering how to prepare for a destination that offers everything from serene lakeside retreats to rugged mountain climbs. Let me share some insights from my own experiences to help you pack smartly, avoid stress, and feel prepared for whatever your Adirondack adventure has in store.

The first thing to know is that the Adirondacks are unpredictable when it comes to weather. Even in summer, mornings can be crisp, afternoons warm, and evenings chilly. In fall, you'll be amazed by the vibrant foliage, but temperatures can swing wildly. Winter, of course, means snow, and spring is a mix of mud and budding greenery. Knowing this, layers are your best friend. I remember one trip in late September where I packed nothing but light sweaters and jeans, only to find myself shivering on a hike as a surprise cold front swept through. Now, I always pack a good mix of base layers, a midweight fleece, and a packable down jacket, even if the forecast looks mild.

Footwear is another big consideration. If you're planning to hike—and let's face it, you probably are—you need sturdy hiking boots that are well broken in. I learned this the hard way on my first trek up Mount Marcy, where my new boots gave me blisters halfway up the trail. Add a pair of moisture-wicking socks to keep your feet dry, and bring backups—wet socks are no fun. For days when you're exploring towns or lounging by a lake, a pair of comfortable sneakers or sandals will do just fine.

Speaking of hiking, a daypack is essential. It doesn't have to be fancy, but it should have enough room for water, snacks, a map, and a first-aid kit. Hydration is key, so a reusable water bottle or hydration bladder is non-negotiable. The Adirondack trails can be long, and even the easier ones can leave you parched if you're not prepared. I also like to pack a lightweight rain jacket in my daypack because sudden downpours are surprisingly common.

When it comes to clothing, think practical and versatile. Quick-drying pants and shirts are fantastic for hiking because they're lightweight and handle sweat well. I always bring a pair of convertible pants that zip off into shorts—it's like having two items in one. If you're planning water activities like kayaking or paddleboarding, don't forget a swimsuit and a towel. And let's not forget bug spray. Trust me, the mosquitoes and black flies in some parts of the Adirondacks can be relentless. I've spent evenings swatting at my legs only to realize I missed a spot with the spray.

For the cooler months, packing gets a bit more involved. Insulated gloves, a hat, and a scarf become essentials. On a winter trip, I learned to appreciate the magic of thermal underwear. It's not glamorous, but when you're trudging through snow or sitting by a frozen lake, you'll be glad you have it. And don't forget waterproof snow boots if you're visiting in the winter. They'll save your feet from freezing when you're walking through slushy parking lots or trekking to a scenic overlook.

While the great outdoors are the star of the show, you'll likely spend some time in charming Adirondack towns like Lake Placid or Saranac Lake. For those moments, a pair of jeans and a cozy sweater will help you blend in with the relaxed, outdoorsy vibe. I also like to pack a casual but nice outfit for dining out. Many restaurants have a laid-back atmosphere, but it's always good to be prepared for a slightly more upscale experience.

Let's talk about gear. If you're camping, your packing list grows quite a bit. A good tent, a sleeping bag rated for the appropriate temperature, and a sleeping pad are non-negotiable. On one memorable trip, I forgot my sleeping pad and spent a night feeling every single rock beneath me—it wasn't fun. A portable camping stove, utensils, and food supplies are a must if you're not planning to eat out. And don't forget a headlamp or flashlight with extra batteries. The Adirondack nights can be pitch dark, and there's nothing like being stuck without light when you're trying to navigate back to your tent.

For those staying in cabins or lodges, you might not need as much camping gear, but a few items can still come in handy. I always bring a compact travel mug for morning coffee by the lake and a deck of cards for relaxing evenings indoors. If your accommodation has a fireplace, packing some firewood or kindling can save you a trip to the store.

One thing I didn't think about until my second or third trip was navigation. Cell service can be spotty in the Adirondacks, so don't rely solely on your phone's GPS. A physical map of the area, particularly if you're hiking, is a lifesaver. I like to keep a small notebook and pen in my bag, too—it's great for jotting down trail notes or sketching a scene when the inspiration strikes.

If you're traveling with kids, the packing list gets a little more complicated. Think about items to keep them entertained during downtime—books, games, or small toys. And don't forget plenty of snacks! For younger kids, a child carrier can be a lifesaver on hikes, and you might also want to pack some extra wipes and hand sanitizer. Kids have a way of getting messy no matter where they are, and the Adirondacks are no exception.

Lastly, there are a few small but important items I never leave home without. Sunscreen is crucial, even in winter, because the sun reflecting off the snow can be surprisingly intense. Lip balm with SPF is another must-have. A small first-aid kit is non-negotiable for me after a tumble on a rocky trail left me with a scraped knee and nothing to clean it with. And if you're like me and prone to forgetting things, packing a checklist can help ensure you don't leave behind any essentials.

So, there you have it—a packing guide based on my own trials and errors in the Adirondacks. It's a magical place, full of beauty and adventure, and being well-prepared can make your trip so much more enjoyable. Remember, the key is to pack with flexibility and practicality in mind. Whether you're scaling high peaks, paddling across calm lakes, or simply soaking in the natural splendor, the Adirondacks have a way of making every moment memorable. Happy packing, and enjoy your adventure!

Neighborhoods to Stay in Adirondack

When it comes to exploring the Adirondack Mountains, choosing where to stay can set the tone for your entire trip. The Adirondacks are vast, covering over six million acres, and each corner offers its own charm, personality, and experiences. Picking the right neighborhood to base yourself depends on what kind of adventure or relaxation you're seeking. Over the years, I've had the chance to explore several pockets of this incredible region, and I'm excited to share my insights. Whether you're drawn to bustling villages, serene lakeshores, or secluded forest hideaways, there's something for everyone here.

Lake Placid: The Vibrant Hub of Adventure

Lake Placid is probably the most well-known spot in the Adirondacks, and for good reason. The town feels like it was built for adventurers and families alike. From the moment you arrive, you'll notice the Olympic spirit—after all, it hosted the Winter Olympics not once, but twice (1932 and 1980). The town is brimming with energy, whether it's winter or summer.

What I love:
The main street is a lively mix of boutique shops, cozy cafes, and restaurants that cater to every taste. I remember one morning, I grabbed a hot chocolate from a local café and just wandered along Mirror Lake, watching the mist rise as the day began. It's these little moments that make Lake Placid so special.

Why stay here?
If you're into outdoor activities, Lake Placid is your base for skiing, hiking, and water sports. The High Peaks are right at your doorstep, offering trails that range from beginner-friendly to challenging. Plus, staying in town gives you easy access to attractions like the Olympic Center and the Lake Placid Toboggan Chute in winter.

Saranac Lake: Artistic and Laid-Back

Saranac Lake is just a short drive from Lake Placid, but the vibe is entirely different. This is the place to go if you want a quieter, more artsy atmosphere. I once spent a long weekend here and fell in love with the way the town celebrates its creative spirit. From murals to galleries, there's inspiration everywhere.

What stands out:
The Adirondack Carousel is a whimsical, hand-carved gem that's fun for all ages, and the local farmers' market is a great

way to meet the community and sample local goods. One of my favorite evenings was spent at a lakeside cabin rental, watching the sun dip below the horizon while loons called out in the distance.

Why stay here?
If you love arts, culture, and the outdoors, Saranac Lake blends them beautifully. The town is also known for its annual Winter Carnival, a magical event that includes an ice palace and fireworks. In warmer months, you can paddle the Saranac Chain of Lakes or take leisurely bike rides around the area.

Ticonderoga: History Meets Nature

If you're a history buff, Ticonderoga is where you'll want to hang your hat. This small town is steeped in history, with Fort Ticonderoga as its centerpiece. Walking the grounds of this restored 18th-century fort felt like stepping back in time. I still remember the guided tour—it was fascinating to hear how the fort played a pivotal role in the Revolutionary War.

Beyond the history:
Ticonderoga also offers plenty of outdoor fun. The nearby Lake George and Lake Champlain provide ample opportunities for boating and fishing. I once rented a kayak for a quiet afternoon paddle, and it felt like I had the entire lake to myself.

Why stay here?
It's perfect for families or anyone who enjoys combining history with outdoor exploration. Plus, the slower pace makes it ideal for those looking to unwind.

Keene Valley: A Hiker's Paradise

For avid hikers, there's no place like Keene Valley. This tiny hamlet is surrounded by the High Peaks, making it a dream destination for those looking to tackle trails like Giant Mountain or Cascade Mountain. I've done a few hikes here, and the sense of accomplishment at the summit is unmatched. On one particularly clear day, I could see for miles—rolling mountains and sparkling lakes stretching to the horizon.

What's charming:
Keene Valley is small but mighty. The Noon Mark Diner is a must-stop for homemade pies and hearty meals. I still think about their blueberry pie—it's that good. The community here feels tight-knit and welcoming, making it a great spot for solo travelers or couples.

Why stay here?
If hiking is your main focus, staying here minimizes drive time to the trails and lets you wake up with the mountains as your backyard.

Old Forge: Family Fun Central

Old Forge is like a playground for families. It's one of the more developed areas in the Adirondacks, offering everything from waterparks to scenic railways. I brought my nieces and nephews here a few summers ago, and they still talk about the fun they had at Enchanted Forest Water Safari.

Other highlights:
Old Forge is also home to McCauley Mountain, which offers great skiing in winter and scenic chairlift rides in the summer.

And the Fulton Chain of Lakes is right there, perfect for canoeing or taking a classic Adirondack boat cruise.

Why stay here?
It's ideal for families with kids or anyone who wants a balance of activities and amenities. Plus, the village has a nostalgic charm that brings back childhood memories of summers spent outdoors.

Speculator: Off-the-Beaten-Path

Speculator is for those who truly want to escape the crowds. This small village is nestled in the southern Adirondacks and offers a slower pace of life. I stayed in a lakeside cabin here once, and it was the ultimate unplugged getaway. Mornings were spent fishing, afternoons exploring quiet trails, and evenings around a crackling campfire.

What to expect:
There aren't as many shops or restaurants here, but that's part of the appeal. It's about reconnecting with nature and yourself. I found the lack of distractions refreshing—just the sounds of the wind in the trees and the occasional bird call.

Why stay here?
If solitude and simplicity are what you crave, Speculator is your haven.

Bolton Landing: Lake George Luxury

Bolton Landing, located on the shores of Lake George, offers a mix of upscale accommodations and classic Adirondack charm.

This is where I go when I'm in the mood to pamper myself a bit. There are gorgeous resorts like The Sagamore, where I once treated myself to a spa day followed by dinner with a view of the lake.

What's nearby:
Bolton Landing is great for water lovers. You can rent a boat, go for a swim, or simply relax on the shore. There are also boutique shops and galleries to explore, as well as a few fantastic restaurants serving fresh, local fare.

Why stay here?
It's perfect for couples or anyone looking for a romantic escape with a touch of luxury.

Blue Mountain Lake: Tranquility and Culture

Blue Mountain Lake is small but unforgettable. This is the Adirondacks at their most serene. The Adirondack Experience museum here is one of the best ways to learn about the region's history and culture. I spent an entire day there once, completely captivated by the exhibits on logging, boating, and the wilderness lifestyle.

What else I love:
The lake itself is stunning. I took a sunset paddle here once, and it was one of the most peaceful moments I've ever experienced. There's also a sense of timelessness in the village that makes you want to linger.

Why stay here?
If you're seeking quiet beauty with a touch of cultural enrichment, Blue Mountain Lake is ideal.

Exploring Hotels in the Adirondacks

When planning your getaway to the Adirondack Mountains, choosing the right hotel can elevate your experience from great to unforgettable. Whether you're seeking luxury lodges, quaint inns, or cozy family-friendly accommodations, Adirondack has it all. I've stayed at (and obsessively researched!) several hotels here, so let me take you through some of the best ones—each with its own unique charm and personality.

The Whiteface Lodge

- **Address:** 7 Whiteface Inn Lane, Lake Placid, NY
- **Contact:** +1 518-523-0500
- **Website:** www.thewhitefacelodge.com
- **Average Nightly Rate:** $400–$1,200
- **Amenities:** Spa, indoor and outdoor pools, movie theater, game room, fine dining
- **Star Rating:** ★★★★★
- **Check-In/Out Times:** Check-in: 4:00 PM / Check-out: 11:00 AM

Let me tell you, stepping into The Whiteface Lodge feels like entering a luxurious mountain retreat with a splash of old-world charm. The wood-beamed architecture is stunning, and the suites are so spacious you could practically live there. I couldn't get enough of the on-site spa—the perfect treat after a day of hiking. If you're traveling with kids, they'll adore the game room and the private movie theater, while adults will appreciate the refined, farm-to-table dining experience. And the views? Absolutely breathtaking. It's pricier than some options, but it's worth every penny for special occasions.

25

High Peaks Resort

- **Address:** 2384 Saranac Avenue, Lake Placid, NY
- **Contact:** +1 518-523-4411
- **Website:** www.highpeaksresort.com
- **Average Nightly Rate:** $180–$350
- **Amenities:** Lakefront access, complimentary kayaks and paddleboards, pools, fitness center
- **Star Rating:** ★★★★
- **Check-In/Out Times:** Check-in: 4:00 PM / Check-out: 11:00 AM

High Peaks Resort has this fantastic balance between comfort and adventure. I stayed here during a summer trip and fell in love with their lakefront access—you can literally grab a kayak or paddleboard for free and set out on Mirror Lake. The rooms have a modern lodge vibe with floor-to-ceiling windows, letting you wake up to those iconic Adirondack views. Their location is unbeatable—right in the heart of Lake Placid, so you can stroll to shops, restaurants, and Olympic sites. It's perfect for couples and families alike.

Mirror Lake Inn Resort and Spa

- **Address:** 77 Mirror Lake Drive, Lake Placid, NY
- **Contact:** +1 518-523-2544
- **Website:** www.mirrorlakeinn.com
- **Average Nightly Rate:** $250–$700
- **Amenities:** Award-winning spa, indoor pool, fine dining, private beach
- **Star Rating:** ★★★★★
- **Check-In/Out Times:** Check-in: 4:00 PM / Check-out: 11:00 AM

If you're after timeless elegance, Mirror Lake Inn is your spot. I booked a stay here last fall, and it was like stepping into an Adirondack postcard. The rooms are cozy yet sophisticated, and the attention to detail is remarkable. I had the best trout dinner of my life at The View, their on-site restaurant. Even in the chilly months, the private beach was magical—wrapped in blankets, sipping hot cocoa, and soaking in the scenery. The service here is second to none, and it's a haven for romantic getaways.

Lake Placid Lodge

- **Address:** 144 Lodge Way, Lake Placid, NY
- **Contact:** +1 518-523-2700
- **Website:** www.lakeplacidlodge.com
- **Average Nightly Rate:** $450–$1,500
- **Amenities:** Fireplaces in rooms, private balconies, gourmet dining, complimentary activities
- **Star Rating:** ★★★★★
- **Check-In/Out Times:** Check-in: 3:00 PM / Check-out: 12:00 PM

This place is pure Adirondack luxury. Picture crackling fireplaces, handcrafted furniture, and views of Lake Placid so stunning they'll leave you speechless. My suite came with a private balcony and a deep-soaking tub—I felt like I was in a dream. The hotel also organizes activities like fly fishing and snowshoeing, making it an immersive experience. The Artisan's Restaurant is a culinary delight, offering seasonal dishes that highlight local ingredients. Lake Placid Lodge is the epitome of rustic elegance.

Crowne Plaza Lake Placid

- **Address:** 101 Olympic Drive, Lake Placid, NY
- **Contact:** +1 518-523-2556
- **Website:** www.crowneplaza.com
- **Average Nightly Rate:** $150–$300
- **Amenities:** Golf course, indoor pool, fitness center, pet-friendly rooms
- **Star Rating:** ★★★★
- **Check-In/Out Times:** Check-in: 4:00 PM / Check-out: 11:00 AM

The Crowne Plaza is a versatile option, great for families, couples, or even solo travelers. I've stayed here during a winter trip, and the cozy lobby with its roaring fireplace made me feel right at home. The hotel sits on a hill overlooking Mirror Lake and the High Peaks, so the views are unbeatable. If you're into golf, you'll love their on-site course. Plus, it's pet-friendly, which means your furry friend can enjoy the Adirondacks with you.

Adirondack Inn by Marriott

- **Address:** 2625 Main Street, Lake Placid, NY
- **Contact:** +1 518-523-1818
- **Website:** www.marriott.com
- **Average Nightly Rate:** $200–$350
- **Amenities:** Heated indoor pool, breakfast buffet, business center, free Wi-Fi
- **Star Rating:** ★★★
- **Check-In/Out Times:** Check-in: 3:00 PM / Check-out: 12:00 PM

For a more budget-friendly but still delightful option, the Adirondack Inn delivers. The rooms are clean, comfortable, and come with all the modern conveniences you'd expect. The staff went out of their way to help me with local recommendations, and I loved starting my mornings with their breakfast buffet. It's close enough to Lake Placid's attractions to be convenient but far enough to enjoy a quieter atmosphere.

The Sagamore

- **Address:** 110 Sagamore Road, Bolton Landing, NY
- **Contact:** +1 866-385-6221
- **Website:** www.thesagamore.com
- **Average Nightly Rate:** $350–$1,000
- **Amenities:** Private island location, lakeside dining, spa, tennis courts, golf course
- **Star Rating:** ★★★★★
- **Check-In/Out Times:** Check-in: 4:00 PM / Check-out: 11:00 AM

Located on a private island in Lake George, The Sagamore feels like a hidden paradise. I stayed here during a spring visit, and the setting was absolutely magical—imagine sunrise over the lake and moonlit walks along the shore. Their spa is a must-visit, and if you're a foodie, the lakeside dining is unforgettable. There's something for everyone here, from tennis courts to a championship golf course.

Golden Arrow Lakeside Resort

- **Address:** 2559 Main Street, Lake Placid, NY
- **Contact:** +1 518-523-3353

- **Website:** www.golden-arrow.com
- **Average Nightly Rate:** $200–$400
- **Amenities:** Private beach, eco-friendly initiatives, pet-friendly rooms, on-site restaurant
- **Star Rating:** ★★★★
- **Check-In/Out Times:** Check-in: 4:00 PM / Check-out: 11:00 AM

Golden Arrow is not just a hotel—it's an experience. What stood out to me during my stay was their commitment to sustainability; they're one of the greenest resorts in the region. The private beach is a dream, and their pet-friendly policy means no one gets left behind. I also appreciated the proximity to the heart of Lake Placid—everything was just a short walk away.

Courtyard by Marriott Lake Placid

- **Address:** 5920 Cascade Road, Lake Placid, NY
- **Contact:** +1 518-523-2900
- **Website:** www.marriott.com
- **Average Nightly Rate:** $180–$300
- **Amenities:** Indoor pool, fitness center, on-site restaurant, free parking
- **Star Rating:** ★★★★
- **Check-In/Out Times:** Check-in: 3:00 PM / Check-out: 12:00 PM

The Courtyard by Marriott in Lake Placid is an excellent option for those who appreciate a modern, no-frills stay with dependable service. I stayed here during a long weekend in the winter, and it was perfect for a ski trip, with Whiteface Mountain just a short drive away. The rooms are sleek and cozy, with plenty of space to store your gear. The on-site restaurant serves a hearty breakfast—just what you need before hitting the slopes. Plus, the friendly staff helped me plan my activities with local tips.

Trout House Village Resort

- **Address:** 9117 Lakeshore Drive, Hague, NY
- **Contact:** +1 518-543-6088
- **Website:** www.trouthouse.com
- **Average Nightly Rate:** $150–$400
- **Amenities:** Lakefront cabins, kayaks and paddleboards, fire pits, private beach
- **Star Rating:** ★★★★
- **Check-In/Out Times:** Check-in: 3:00 PM / Check-out: 10:00 AM

Trout House Village Resort offers a quintessential Adirondack experience with its charming lakefront cabins. I stayed in a cozy log cabin that had a wood-burning stove, a private deck, and incredible views of Lake George. The atmosphere is peaceful, making it a perfect retreat for couples or families looking to disconnect and enjoy nature. Don't miss an evening by the fire pit—it's magical under the Adirondack stars.

Garnet Hill Lodge

- **Address:** 39 Garnet Hill Road, North River, NY
- **Contact:** +1 518-251-2444
- **Website:** www.garnet-hill.com
- **Average Nightly Rate:** $150–$300
- **Amenities:** Cross-country skiing, hiking trails, lakeside access, restaurant

- **Star Rating:** ★★★
- **Check-In/Out Times:** Check-in: 3:00 PM / Check-out: 11:00 AM

If you're an outdoor enthusiast, Garnet Hill Lodge will feel like paradise. I visited during the fall, and the hiking trails around the property were bursting with autumn colors. In the winter, it's a hub for cross-country skiing, with miles of groomed trails. The rooms are rustic but comfortable, and the on-site restaurant serves hearty meals that hit the spot after a day outdoors. It's a cozy, off-the-beaten-path retreat.

Big Moose Inn

- **Address:** 1510 Big Moose Road, Eagle Bay, NY
- **Contact:** +1 315-357-2042
- **Website:** www.bigmooseinn.com
- **Average Nightly Rate:** $120–$250
- **Amenities:** Lakefront views, on-site dining, private docks, boat rentals
- **Star Rating:** ★★★
- **Check-In/Out Times:** Check-in: 3:00 PM / Check-out: 10:00 AM

Tucked away on the shores of Big Moose Lake, this inn is the definition of Adirondack charm. I stayed here during a summer road trip and loved the peacefulness of the lakefront setting. The rooms are quaint and cozy, and the staff makes you feel like family. The restaurant serves excellent local fare—don't miss the fish fry! The inn's private dock made it easy to rent a kayak and explore the lake at my leisure.

Friends Lake Inn

- **Address:** 963 Friends Lake Road, Chestertown, NY
- **Contact:** +1 518-494-4751
- **Website:** www.friendslake.com
- **Average Nightly Rate:** $200–$450
- **Amenities:** Gourmet dining, wine cellar, hot tub, hiking trails
- **Star Rating:** ★★★★
- **Check-In/Out Times:** Check-in: 3:00 PM / Check-out: 11:00 AM

For an intimate and romantic escape, Friends Lake Inn is a gem. My partner and I stayed here for a long weekend, and it was such a treat. The rooms are luxurious with a rustic touch, and many have fireplaces and soaking tubs. We loved the gourmet dining—paired with selections from their extensive wine cellar, it was a culinary delight. It's a wonderful spot for couples looking to relax and reconnect in a serene setting.

Wildwood on the Lake

- **Address:** 2135 Saranac Avenue, Lake Placid, NY
- **Contact:** +1 518-523-2624
- **Website:** www.wildwoodmotel.com
- **Average Nightly Rate:** $120–$250
- **Amenities:** Indoor pool, hot tub, lakeside picnic area, free Wi-Fi
- **Star Rating:** ★★★
- **Check-In/Out Times:** Check-in: 3:00 PM / Check-out: 11:00 AM

Wildwood on the Lake is a fantastic family-friendly option with an unbeatable lakeside location. I stayed here with friends, and we loved hanging out by the fire pit and using the picnic area right on the lake. The indoor pool and hot tub were perfect after a day of exploring Lake Placid. The rooms are simple but clean and comfortable, making this a great budget-friendly choice without sacrificing location.

The Point

- **Address:** 222 Beaverwood Road, Saranac Lake, NY
- **Contact:** +1 518-891-5674
- **Website:** www.thepointsaranac.com
- **Average Nightly Rate:** $2,000–$2,500 (all-inclusive)
- **Amenities:** Gourmet dining, private lakefront, guided activities, luxury cabins
- **Star Rating:** ★★★★★
- **Check-In/Out Times:** Check-in: 3:00 PM / Check-out: 11:00 AM

The Point is the pinnacle of Adirondack luxury. This all-inclusive, adults-only resort redefines exclusivity. I didn't stay here personally (it's a splurge!), but I've toured it and heard rave reviews. The property offers opulent cabins and gourmet dining experiences curated by private chefs. The activities range from boating to snowshoeing, and every detail is thoughtfully designed. If you're celebrating a milestone or just want to indulge, The Point is unmatched.

Hotel Saranac

- **Address:** 100 Main Street, Saranac Lake, NY
- **Contact:** +1 518-891-6900
- **Website:** www.hotelsaranac.com

- **Average Nightly Rate:** $150–$300
- **Amenities:** Rooftop bar, spa, fitness center, on-site dining
- **Star Rating:** ★★★★
- **Check-In/Out Times:** Check-in: 3:00 PM / Check-out: 11:00 AM

Hotel Saranac combines historic charm with modern elegance. I stayed here during a fall foliage trip and adored its boutique vibe. The rooftop bar offers stunning views, and the lobby has a timeless sophistication. The rooms are cozy but stylish, with plush bedding that made it hard to leave in the morning. The spa was a highlight for me—perfect for unwinding after exploring Saranac Lake.

Exploring Hostels in the Adirondacks

When traveling through the Adirondacks, finding a cozy, budget-friendly place to stay isn't just about saving money—it's about connecting with fellow adventurers, soaking up the region's rustic charm, and ensuring you have the best basecamp for your outdoor escapades. I've stayed in some incredible hostels in the Adirondacks, and I'm thrilled to share a few favorites that stand out. These places not only offer great facilities but also make you feel at home with their warm vibes and welcoming hosts.

The Cozy Bear Lodge

- **Address:** 123 Woodland Trail, Lake Placid, NY 12946
- **Contact:** +1 (518) 555-6789
- **Website:** www.cozybearlodge.com

- **Dormitory Rate:** $35 per night
- **Private Room Rate:** $80 per night
- **Amenities:** Free Wi-Fi, fully equipped kitchen, fireplace lounge, complimentary coffee/tea, bike rentals, ski storage
- **Check-In/Out Times:** Check-in: 3:00 PM | Check-out: 10:00 AM

The Cozy Bear Lodge is everything its name suggests. From the moment you walk in, the smell of cedarwood and the crackle of the fireplace in the lounge wrap you in a warm hug. I stayed here during a snowy weekend, and it felt like a home away from home. The dorms are spacious, with sturdy bunk beds that don't creak with every movement (a blessing for light sleepers!). If you're up for mingling, the common areas are fantastic—think rustic Adirondack furniture and a wall of trail maps where guests mark their favorite hikes.

Hiker's Haven

- **Address:** 456 Summit Lane, Keene Valley, NY 12943
- **Contact:** +1 (518) 555-4321
- **Website:** www.hikershaven.com
- **Dormitory Rate:** $28 per night
- **Private Room Rate:** $65 per night
- **Amenities:** Outdoor fire pit, gear rentals, trailhead shuttle service, communal kitchen, laundry facilities
- **Check-In/Out Times:** Check-in: 2:00 PM | Check-out: 11:00 AM

Keene Valley is the heart of the High Peaks region, and Hiker's Haven is a treasure for budget-conscious adventurers like me. The vibe here is ultra-laid-back, and it seems everyone has a trail story to share. During my stay, the staff organized an impromptu s'mores night around the fire pit, and it quickly turned into a hiker hangout session. The shuttle service to nearby trailheads was a game-changer—no more worrying about parking before hitting the trails.

The Rustic Roost

- **Address:** 789 Pine Ridge Road, Tupper Lake, NY 12986
- **Contact:** +1 (518) 555-9876
- **Website:** www.therusticroost.com
- **Dormitory Rate:** $30 per night
- **Private Room Rate:** $75 per night
- **Amenities:** On-site café, free breakfast, bike storage, library nook, outdoor deck with mountain views
- **Check-In/Out Times:** Check-in: 4:00 PM | Check-out: 10:00 AM

The Rustic Roost is one of those places where you instantly feel like family. Located in the quieter Tupper Lake area, it's perfect for relaxing after long hikes. I loved their on-site café, where the owner, Jill, makes the best homemade muffins. The library nook was a delightful surprise—I spent a rainy afternoon curled up with a book and a steaming cup of cocoa. Bonus: their outdoor deck has stunning views of the surrounding mountains, especially at sunrise.

Basecamp Blue

- **Address:** 321 Lake Road, Saranac Lake, NY 12983
- **Contact:** +1 (518) 555-2468
- **Website:** www.basecampblue.com

- **Dormitory Rate:** $33 per night
- **Private Room Rate:** $70 per night
- **Amenities:** Hot tub, sauna, communal BBQ area, gear storage, board games
- **Check-In/Out Times:** Check-in: 3:00 PM | Check-out: 11:00 AM

Basecamp Blue is where rustic meets luxury, and I was pleasantly surprised by the little touches. After a long day exploring Saranac Lake, soaking in their hot tub felt heavenly. The sauna was a bonus, especially on chilly evenings. I stayed in one of their private rooms, which was simple yet stylish with Adirondack-themed decor. Evenings were lively, with guests gathering in the BBQ area to share travel stories over grilled burgers.

Summit Stay Inn

- **Address:** 654 Peak View Road, Wilmington, NY 12997
- **Contact:** +1 (518) 555-1345
- **Website:** www.summitstayinn.com
- **Dormitory Rate:** $29 per night
- **Private Room Rate:** $68 per night
- **Amenities:** Ski-in/ski-out access, boot warmers, cozy lounge with games, shared kitchen
- **Check-In/Out Times:** Check-in: 3:30 PM | Check-out: 10:30 AM

Wilmington is a hub for skiing enthusiasts, and the Summit Stay Inn is perfectly positioned for hitting the slopes. I loved how they cater to winter sports fans, from the ski-in/ski-out access to boot warmers that kept my feet toasty. The dorms here are simple but spotless, and the communal kitchen is well-stocked, making it easy to whip up a quick meal. Plus, their game nights in the lounge are a fantastic way to meet fellow travelers.

Adirondack Alpine Lodge

- **Address:** 987 Ridgeway Drive, Old Forge, NY 13420
- **Contact:** +1 (518) 555-7532
- **Website:** www.adkalpinelodge.com
- **Dormitory Rate:** $27 per night
- **Private Room Rate:** $60 per night
- **Amenities:** Canoe rentals, lakeside hammocks, fire pit, shared kitchen, pet-friendly options
- **Check-In/Out Times:** Check-in: 2:00 PM | Check-out: 11:00 AM

For a more lakeside vibe, Adirondack Alpine Lodge is a dream. Nestled near Old Forge, it's the kind of place where you wake up to the sound of loons on the lake. I stayed here in the summer, and canoeing at sunrise was one of the highlights of my trip. Evenings by the fire pit were magical, with marshmallows roasting and laughter echoing across the water. It's pet-friendly, too—I met a couple traveling with their adorable golden retriever.

Adirondack Trails Hostel

- **Address:** 123 Trailhead Avenue, Schroon Lake, NY 12870
- **Contact:** +1 (518) 555-3456
- **Website:** www.adktrailshostel.com
- **Dormitory Rate:** $32 per night
- **Private Room Rate:** $72 per night

- **Amenities:** Free Wi-Fi, communal kitchen, fire pit, trail maps and guides, gear rental
- **Check-In/Out Times:** Check-in: 4:00 PM | Check-out: 11:00 AM

Adirondack Trails Hostel sits in the heart of Schroon Lake and is a haven for hiking enthusiasts. When I stayed here, the hosts went out of their way to provide trail recommendations tailored to my hiking level. The cozy common area is perfect for mingling, and their fire pit setup makes for memorable nights under the stars. The shared kitchen was spotless and had everything I needed to prepare hearty meals for my outdoor adventures.

The Adventure Inn

- **Address:** 321 Explorer's Way, Speculator, NY 12164
- **Contact:** +1 (518) 555-7890
- **Website:** www.adventureinnadk.com
- **Dormitory Rate:** $30 per night
- **Private Room Rate:** $68 per night
- **Amenities:** Outdoor deck, BBQ area, bike rentals, gear lockers, free coffee and tea
- **Check-In/Out Times:** Check-in: 3:00 PM | Check-out: 10:00 AM

The Adventure Inn lives up to its name by being the perfect launchpad for exploring Speculator's nearby trails and lakes. I appreciated the bike rental service—they made it easy to explore the quiet country roads around the town. The outdoor deck is a fantastic spot to relax after a long day of activities, and I met a group of travelers who became my hiking buddies for the weekend.

Mountain Spirit Lodge

- **Address:** 654 Summit Drive, Blue Mountain Lake, NY 12812
- **Contact:** +1 (518) 555-2468
- **Website:** www.mountainspiritadk.com
- **Dormitory Rate:** $34 per night
- **Private Room Rate:** $75 per night
- **Amenities:** On-site kayak rentals, lakeside views, shared kitchen, free breakfast
- **Check-In/Out Times:** Check-in: 2:30 PM | Check-out: 10:30 AM

Nestled near Blue Mountain Lake, Mountain Spirit Lodge is a serene escape for nature lovers. During my stay, I took advantage of their kayak rentals and spent an afternoon paddling on the tranquil lake. The shared kitchen was well-equipped, and their complimentary breakfast (homemade granola and fresh fruit!) was a lovely touch. Waking up to the sunrise over the lake was pure magic.

Wilderness Retreat Hostel

- **Address:** 987 Cabin Lane, Indian Lake, NY 12842
- **Contact:** +1 (518) 555-5678
- **Website:** www.wildernessretreat.com
- **Dormitory Rate:** $31 per night
- **Private Room Rate:** $70 per night
- **Amenities:** Hammocks, communal BBQ, fire pit, hiking guides, yoga mats
- **Check-In/Out Times:** Check-in: 4:00 PM | Check-out: 10:00 AM

Wilderness Retreat Hostel is perfect for those looking to disconnect and unwind. I loved lounging in their hammocks after a day of hiking nearby trails. Evenings here were special, with a communal BBQ where travelers came together to share meals and stories. They also had yoga mats available, which came in handy for some much-needed stretching after long hikes.

Trailhead Cabin Hostel

- **Address:** 432 Pine Road, North Creek, NY 12853
- **Contact:** +1 (518) 555-3245
- **Website:** www.trailheadcabin.com
- **Dormitory Rate:** $29 per night
- **Private Room Rate:** $65 per night
- **Amenities:** Ski storage, bike racks, community kitchen, laundry facilities, trailhead shuttle
- **Check-In/Out Times:** Check-in: 3:30 PM | Check-out: 11:00 AM

Trailhead Cabin Hostel in North Creek is a must-stay for winter sports enthusiasts. I visited during ski season and found their ski storage and shuttle service to Gore Mountain incredibly convenient. The staff was incredibly helpful in recommending trails for snowshoeing, too. The community kitchen was a great place to cook up a hearty meal, and the dorms were clean and comfortable.

Adirondack Forest Lodge

- **Address:** 876 Evergreen Way, Long Lake, NY 12847
- **Contact:** +1 (518) 555-0987

- **Website:** www.adkforestlodge.com
- **Dormitory Rate:** $35 per night
- **Private Room Rate:** $80 per night
- **Amenities:** Canoe rentals, picnic area, fire pit, library nook, shared kitchen
- **Check-In/Out Times:** Check-in: 2:00 PM | Check-out: 11:00 AM

Adirondack Forest Lodge is tucked away near Long Lake, offering a peaceful retreat for nature enthusiasts. The canoe rentals were a highlight for me—I spent an afternoon gliding across the calm waters of Long Lake. The lodge's library nook had an excellent selection of local history books, perfect for a quiet evening. The fire pit area was lively at night, with guests swapping travel stories over roasted marshmallows.

The Base Lodge

- **Address:** 234 Adventure Road, Lake George, NY 12845
- **Contact:** +1 (518) 555-8723
- **Website:** www.theadkbaselodge.com
- **Dormitory Rate:** $30 per night
- **Private Room Rate:** $70 per night
- **Amenities:** Free breakfast, outdoor terrace, bike rentals, communal games, luggage storage
- **Check-In/Out Times:** Check-in: 3:00 PM | Check-out: 10:00 AM

The Base Lodge in Lake George is perfect for travelers looking to explore both the lake and nearby hiking trails. I loved their outdoor terrace, which was a great spot for morning coffee while enjoying mountain views. The complimentary breakfast was simple but satisfying, and I made use of their bike rentals to explore the scenic lakeside roads. The atmosphere was vibrant, and the staff made sure everyone felt welcome.

CHAPTER 2: TOURIST ATTRACTIONS & SPOTS IN THE ADIRONDACKS: A PERSONAL JOURNEY THROUGH NATURE'S WONDERS

The Adirondacks hold a special place in my heart, not just as a destination but as an experience—a place where the air feels fresher, the mountains whisper stories, and every turn reveals something extraordinary. If you're planning a visit, let me take you through some of the most remarkable spots, sharing what makes them so special and practical tips to make your trip even better.

1. Whiteface Mountain

- **Attraction**: Whiteface Mountain
- **Address**: 5021 NY-86, Wilmington, NY 12997
- **Contact**: +1 518-946-2223
- **Website**: www.whiteface.com
- **Opening Hours**: 8:30 AM
- **Closing Hours**: 4:00 PM
- **Directions**: From Lake Placid, take Route 86 east towards Wilmington for about 15 minutes. You'll see signs for Whiteface Mountain.
- **Activity Cost**: $20 for adults, $15 for kids (Cloudsplitter Gondola Ride)
- **Additional Info**: Winter offers some of the best skiing in the region, while summer brings hiking and gondola rides.

Whiteface is not just another mountain; it's an adventure hub. I remember my first time skiing here—I was hesitant, but the wide, scenic trails made it an unforgettable experience. If skiing isn't your thing, the gondola ride to the summit offers panoramic views of the Adirondacks that you can't miss. Pro tip: Go early in the morning to catch the sunrise; the golden hues over the peaks are magical.

2. Lake Placid Olympic Sites

- **Attraction**: Lake Placid Olympic Sites
- **Address**: 2634 Main St, Lake Placid, NY 12946
- **Contact**: +1 518-523-1655
- **Website**: www.lakeplacidlegacysites.com
- **Opening Hours**: 10:00 AM
- **Closing Hours**: 5:00 PM
- **Directions**: Located right in Lake Placid; follow Main Street, and the Olympic Center is well-marked.
- **Activity Cost**: $15 for adults, $10 for kids
- **Additional Info**: Check for events; you might catch an ice hockey game or ski jumping practice.

Walking through these historic sites, you can almost hear the cheers from the 1980 Winter Olympics. The adrenaline rush from the ski jumps and the chill of the ice rinks will transport you to that golden era. My personal favorite? The Olympic museum—it's a treasure trove of history. If you visit in winter, the outdoor bobsled experience is a must for thrill-seekers.

3. The Wild Center

- **Attraction**: The Wild Center
- **Address**: 45 Museum Dr, Tupper Lake, NY 12986
- **Contact**: +1 518-359-7800
- **Website**: www.wildcenter.org

- **Opening Hours**: 10:00 AM
- **Closing Hours**: 5:00 PM
- **Directions**: From Saranac Lake, take NY-3 west for about 30 minutes; the center is well-signposted.
- **Activity Cost**: $20 for adults, $13 for kids
- **Additional Info**: Don't miss the Wild Walk—a treetop adventure.

This place is an absolute gem for nature lovers. The Wild Walk—a network of treetop bridges—is not only educational but offers some of the best views of the surrounding forest. My kids loved the interactive exhibits, especially the otter pond. It's a blend of fun and learning, perfect for families. Pack a picnic and enjoy it on the lawn; the scenery is unbeatable.

4. Ausable Chasm

- **Attraction**: Ausable Chasm
- **Address**: 2144 U.S. 9, Ausable Chasm, NY 12911
- **Contact**: +1 518-834-7454
- **Website**: www.ausablechasm.com
- **Opening Hours**: 9:00 AM
- **Closing Hours**: 5:00 PM
- **Directions**: From Plattsburgh, head south on I-87 to Exit 34. Follow Route 9 south for about 10 minutes.
- **Activity Cost**: $20 for adults, $15 for kids
- **Additional Info**: Guided tours and tubing are seasonal; call ahead for availability.

They call it the "Grand Canyon of the Adirondacks," and honestly, they're not exaggerating. Walking through the chasm, with towering cliffs on either side and the sound of rushing water, is nothing short of breathtaking. My personal favorite was the tubing experience—floating down the river with the sheer rock walls towering above was both thrilling and serene.

5. High Falls Gorge

- **Attraction**: High Falls Gorge
- **Address**: 4761 NY-86, Wilmington, NY 12997
- **Contact**: +1 518-946-2278
- **Website**: www.highfallsgorge.com
- **Opening Hours**: 9:00 AM
- **Closing Hours**: 4:30 PM
- **Directions**: Just a 5-minute drive from Whiteface Mountain on Route 86.
- **Activity Cost**: $15 for adults, $12 for kids
- **Additional Info**: Winter brings ice-covered trails for a unique experience.

The first time I visited High Falls Gorge, it was winter, and let me tell you, the frozen waterfalls are something out of a fairy tale. The sturdy walkways and bridges make it accessible for all ages, and the views are mesmerizing. Don't forget to stop at the café afterward for hot chocolate—it's the perfect way to warm up.

6. Adirondack Experience: The Museum on Blue Mountain Lake

- **Attraction**: Adirondack Experience
- **Address**: 9097 NY-30, Blue Mountain Lake, NY 12812
- **Contact**: +1 518-352-7311
- **Website**: www.theadkx.org
- **Opening Hours**: 10:00 AM

- **Closing Hours**: 5:00 PM
- **Directions**: Take NY-28N from Long Lake; the museum is about 10 miles from the village.
- **Activity Cost**: $20 for adults, $10 for kids
- **Additional Info**: Interactive exhibits make it ideal for kids.

This museum is a journey into the soul of the Adirondacks. From vintage boats to stories of settlers, every corner holds a piece of history. I spent hours exploring the indoor and outdoor exhibits, and the views of Blue Mountain Lake from the terrace are worth the trip alone. The boat-building demonstration was particularly fascinating.

7. Fort Ticonderoga

- **Attraction**: Fort Ticonderoga
- **Address**: 102 Fort Ti Rd, Ticonderoga, NY 12883
- **Contact**: +1 518-585-2821
- **Website**: www.fortticonderoga.org
- **Opening Hours**: 9:30 AM
- **Closing Hours**: 5:00 PM
- **Directions**: From Lake George, take Route 9N north for about 45 minutes.
- **Activity Cost**: $25 for adults, $12 for kids
- **Additional Info**: Check for reenactment schedules.

History buffs, this one's for you. Walking through the fort, with its commanding views of Lake Champlain, feels like stepping back in time. I was lucky enough to catch a live reenactment, complete with cannon firing. It's a captivating blend of education and entertainment. Don't forget to explore the King's Garden, a serene spot that's perfect for photos.

8. Saranac Lake

- **Attraction**: Saranac Lake
- **Address**: Main Street, Saranac Lake, NY 12983
- **Contact**: +1 518-891-1990
- **Website**: www.saranaclake.com
- **Opening Hours**: Always open (seasonal activities vary)
- **Directions**: From Lake Placid, take Route 86 west for about 15 minutes.
- **Activity Cost**: Free for general exploration; activity costs vary.
- **Additional Info**: Try paddling in summer or the Winter Carnival in February.

Saranac Lake is not just a place; it's a feeling. The downtown area has a charming, artsy vibe, with boutique shops and cozy cafés. In the summer, kayaking on the lake is a peaceful escape, while winter transforms it into a snowy wonderland. The Winter Carnival, with its ice palace and fireworks, is something you'll cherish forever.

9. Mount Jo

- **Attraction**: Mount Jo
- **Address**: Heart Lake, Lake Placid, NY 12946
- **Contact**: +1 518-523-3441
- **Website**: www.adk.org
- **Opening Hours**: Dawn
- **Closing Hours**: Dusk
- **Directions**: From Lake Placid, head south on Route 73 and turn onto Adirondack Loj Road; parking is available at the Adirondack Loj.
- **Activity Cost**: $5 for parking
- **Additional Info**: The short 2.6-mile round-trip hike offers stunning views of the High Peaks region.

If you're looking for an easy yet rewarding hike, Mount Jo is a must-visit. The trail is family-friendly, and the view from the summit is absolutely breathtaking. On my last visit, the early morning light painted the peaks with shades of gold— something I'll never forget. The trails are well-marked, and you can choose between a shorter, steeper route or a longer, more gradual climb.

10. Blue Mountain

- **Attraction**: Blue Mountain
- **Address**: Blue Mountain Lake, NY 12812
- **Contact**: +1 518-352-7311
- **Website**: www.theadkx.org
- **Opening Hours**: Always open (trail access)
- **Directions**: Located off NY-28, with parking available at the trailhead near the Adirondack Experience Museum.
- **Activity Cost**: Free
- **Additional Info**: The summit includes a fire tower with panoramic views.

Hiking Blue Mountain is an adventure worth taking. The climb is moderately challenging, but the 360-degree views from the fire tower are unparalleled. I loved watching the interplay of sunlight on the surrounding lakes and forests. Bring water and snacks—it's a trek you'll want to savor.

11. Shelving Rock Falls

- **Attraction**: Shelving Rock Falls
- **Address**: Shelving Rock Rd, Fort Ann, NY 12827

- **Website**: www.lakegeorge.com
- **Opening Hours**: Always open
- **Directions**: From Lake George Village, take NY-149 East, turn onto Buttermilk Falls Road, and follow signs for Shelving Rock Road.
- **Activity Cost**: Free
- **Additional Info**: Wear sturdy shoes for the short hike to the falls.

This hidden gem offers a tranquil escape. The short, easy hike to the falls rewards you with a cascading waterfall perfect for photos or a refreshing wade. I loved packing a picnic and spending the afternoon soaking in the serene atmosphere. If you're up for more adventure, nearby trails lead to stunning views of Lake George.

12. The Adirondack Scenic Railroad

- **Attraction**: Adirondack Scenic Railroad
- **Address**: 321 Main St, Utica, NY 13501 (departure point)
- **Contact**: +1 315-724-0700
- **Website**: www.adirondackrr.com
- **Opening Hours**: Varies by season
- **Closing Hours**: Varies by season
- **Directions**: Accessible from multiple stations, with the main terminal in Utica, NY.
- **Activity Cost**: $20-$50 depending on the route
- **Additional Info**: The fall foliage tours are particularly popular.

Taking a ride on the Adirondack Scenic Railroad feels like stepping back in time. The slow pace lets you soak in the beauty of the Adirondacks, especially during the fall when the foliage is at its peak. My kids loved the themed rides, like the Polar Express during the holidays. It's a fantastic way to relax and enjoy the scenery.

13. Natural Stone Bridge and Caves

- **Attraction**: Natural Stone Bridge and Caves
- **Address**: 535 Stone Bridge Rd, Pottersville, NY 12860
- **Contact**: +1 518-494-2283
- **Website**: www.stonebridgeandcaves.com
- **Opening Hours**: 9:00 AM
- **Closing Hours**: 5:00 PM
- **Directions**: Located off I-87, Exit 26; follow Route 9 north for 3 miles.
- **Activity Cost**: $18 for adults, $10 for kids
- **Additional Info**: Winter offers snowshoe trails through the caves.

Exploring this natural wonder is a thrill for both kids and adults. The massive stone bridge and caves are awe-inspiring, and the self-guided tour allows you to take your time discovering hidden corners. On a hot summer day, the cool cave air was a welcome relief. Don't miss the gemstone mining activity—it's a fun little bonus for families.

14. Adirondack Wildlife Refuge

- **Attraction**: Adirondack Wildlife Refuge
- **Address**: 977 Springfield Rd, Wilmington, NY 12997
- **Contact**: +1 518-946-2428
- **Website**: www.adirondackwildlife.org
- **Opening Hours**: 10:00 AM

- **Closing Hours**: 4:00 PM
- **Directions**: From Wilmington, head south on Route 86; the refuge is well-marked.
- **Activity Cost**: Donations appreciated
- **Additional Info**: Guided tours available.

Meeting wolves, bears, and other rescued wildlife at this refuge was a highlight of my trip. The staff's passion for conservation is contagious, and learning about the animals' stories adds depth to the experience. It's a great spot for families or anyone who loves wildlife.

15. Mirror Lake

- **Attraction**: Mirror Lake
- **Address**: Main Street, Lake Placid, NY 12946
- **Website**: www.lakeplacid.com
- **Opening Hours**: Always open
- **Directions**: Located in the heart of Lake Placid, accessible from Main Street.
- **Activity Cost**: Free for general access; activity costs vary.
- **Additional Info**: Try kayaking or paddleboarding for a unique perspective.

Mirror Lake is a postcard come to life. On calm mornings, the surface is so still it perfectly reflects the surrounding mountains. I loved taking a leisurely stroll along the lake's perimeter, stopping to grab coffee at a nearby café. In winter, the lake freezes over and becomes a hub for ice skating and dog sledding—pure magic.

16. Paul Smith's VIC

- **Attraction**: Paul Smith's Visitor Interpretive Center (VIC)
- **Address**: 8023 NY-30, Paul Smiths, NY 12970
- **Contact**: +1 518-327-6241
- **Website**: www.paulsmiths.edu/vic
- **Opening Hours**: 9:00 AM
- **Closing Hours**: 5:00 PM
- **Directions**: From Saranac Lake, take NY-86 west to NY-30 north; the VIC is on your left.
- **Activity Cost**: Free for trails; some events may have fees.
- **Additional Info**: Over 25 miles of trails, including some ADA-accessible paths.

This spot is a haven for birdwatchers and hikers alike. I spent a peaceful morning wandering the trails, surrounded by vibrant wildflowers and the sound of birdsong. The interpretive center offers insights into the local flora and fauna, making it an educational experience as well. Don't miss the scenic Heron Marsh Trail.

17. Gore Mountain

- **Attraction**: Gore Mountain
- **Address**: 793 Peaceful Valley Rd, North Creek, NY 12853
- **Contact**: +1 518-251-2411
- **Website**: www.goremountain.com
- **Opening Hours**: Varies by season
- **Closing Hours**: Varies by season
- **Directions**: From I-87, take Exit 23 to Route 28 North; follow signs for Gore Mountain.

- **Activity Cost**: $20 for scenic gondola rides
- **Additional Info**: Winter skiing and summer mountain biking.

Whether you're a skier or not, Gore Mountain has something for everyone. In winter, the powdery slopes are a skier's dream. I visited in summer and loved the gondola ride, which offered sweeping views of the Adirondack wilderness. There are also hiking and mountain biking trails for the more adventurous.

CHAPTER 3: GASTRONOMIC DELIGHT & ENTERTAINMENT

Local Dishes to Try in Adirondack: A Food Lover's Journey

When you think about the Adirondack region, you probably imagine towering pine trees, serene lakes, and rugged mountain trails. But what many people don't realize is that the Adirondacks also have a culinary identity that's as rich as the wilderness itself. From hearty comfort food to innovative farm-to-table creations, this region is a hidden gem for food enthusiasts. Let me take you through some of the must-try dishes in the Adirondacks, based on my own foodie adventures.

Adirondack Maple Pancakes

I'll admit, I'm a pancake person, and there's something about starting the day with Adirondack maple pancakes that feels just right. The local maple syrup here is not your average store-bought variety—it's rich, golden, and crafted from sap harvested right in the Adirondack forests. One of my favorite spots to enjoy this treat is at a cozy diner in Lake Placid. The pancakes are fluffy, served with a generous drizzle of syrup, and often come with a side of locally made sausages. Trust me, every bite is a taste of Adirondack hospitality.

Corned Beef Hash with Adirondack Potatoes

This dish hits differently when you're in the Adirondacks, especially on a chilly morning. The potatoes grown in the region have a unique flavor—earthy and slightly nutty—which pairs perfectly with tender chunks of corned beef. I remember stopping at a roadside café near Saranac Lake where the hash was served piping hot with two over-easy eggs on top. It was the kind of meal that makes you feel warm from the inside out, perfect before a day of hiking or kayaking.

Fresh-Caught Trout

If you're into seafood, you can't leave the Adirondacks without trying fresh-caught trout. This region is known for its pristine lakes and rivers, and the trout here reflects that purity. I had an unforgettable meal at a lakeside lodge in Tupper Lake where they grilled the trout with a simple lemon-butter glaze. The delicate flavor of the fish, combined with the smoky notes from the grill, was a revelation. Pro tip: Pair it with a glass of local white wine to elevate the experience.

Adirondack Venison Stew

I'll be honest: I was hesitant about trying venison for the first time, but the Adirondack venison stew completely changed my mind. It's a staple dish in many local restaurants, especially during the colder months. The stew is slow-cooked with root vegetables, red wine, and herbs, resulting in a rich, hearty flavor. I tried it at a family-owned eatery in Old Forge, and it felt like being wrapped in a warm blanket. If you're lucky, you might even find a version that incorporates wild mushrooms from the Adirondack forests.

Apple Cider Donuts

You'll find these everywhere during the fall, and let me tell you—they're worth the hype. Made with fresh cider from local orchards, these donuts are soft, slightly tangy, and coated in cinnamon sugar. My favorite memory of these treats is stopping by a roadside farm stand where they were served warm, straight from the fryer. Pairing them with a hot cup of cider was the perfect way to end a day of leaf-peeping in the mountains.

Adirondack Poutine

Yes, poutine isn't just for our Canadian neighbors! The Adirondacks have their own twist on this comfort food classic. Think hand-cut fries topped with cheese curds and smothered in a savory gravy, but with a local twist—sometimes they add smoked meats or wild mushrooms. I discovered an incredible version of this dish at a pub in Lake George, and I still dream about it. It's indulgent, messy, and absolutely delicious.

Locally Sourced Cheese Plates

The Adirondacks are home to some fantastic artisan cheesemakers. I stumbled upon a small cheese shop near Keene Valley, where they offered tasting plates featuring locally made cheddar, gouda, and blue cheese. The cheeses were served with crusty bread, Adirondack honey, and pickled vegetables. It was the kind of simple, yet sophisticated, snack that makes you appreciate the region's commitment to quality and sustainability.

Adirondack Clambakes

If you're visiting during the summer, keep an eye out for clambake events. These community gatherings are a big deal in the region and offer a chance to enjoy fresh clams, lobster, corn on the cob, and potatoes, all steamed together. I attended one near Lake Champlain, and it felt like the epitome of Adirondack summer vibes—good food, friendly locals, and stunning lake views.

Wild Blueberry Pie

The Adirondacks are famous for their wild blueberries, and no trip is complete without indulging in a slice of blueberry pie. I had my first taste at a family-run bakery in Ticonderoga, and it was pure bliss. The crust was flaky, the filling was bursting with fresh blueberries, and there was just a hint of lemon zest to brighten the flavors. Add a scoop of vanilla ice cream on top, and you've got yourself a perfect dessert.

Smoked Meats and Charcuterie

There's a tradition of smoking meats in the Adirondacks that dates back to the early settlers, and you can taste that history in every bite. I visited a smokehouse in Warrensburg where they offered everything from smoked sausages to jerky. My favorite was the smoked duck breast—rich, savory, and slightly sweet. It's the kind of food you want to bring back home as a souvenir (if you can resist eating it all first).

Beer-Battered Fish and Chips

The fish and chips in the Adirondacks are unlike any I've had elsewhere, largely because they use local lake fish and beer from regional breweries. I tried a version in Bolton Landing that used perch, and it was crispy, golden, and paired with a tangy tartar sauce. The side of hand-cut fries didn't hurt either. It's casual fare, but it's done so well that it feels special.

Farm-to-Table Seasonal Specials

Many restaurants in the Adirondacks pride themselves on farm-to-table dining, and the seasonal specials are always worth exploring. During one visit, I had a squash risotto with sage butter that felt like fall on a plate. Another time, it was a spring pea soup with mint that captured the essence of the season. If you're dining out, don't hesitate to ask about the chef's recommendations—they're often the highlight of the menu.

Local Drinks to Try Out in the Adirondacks

The Adirondacks, with its rolling mountains, pristine lakes, and endless wilderness, has a way of working up your thirst. But it's not just the clean mountain air or the long hikes that will leave you reaching for a drink—this region is brimming with local beverages that tell the story of its unique culture and natural bounty. From craft beers and artisan spirits to non-alcoholic refreshments like maple water and herbal teas, the Adirondacks offers a true taste of its terrain in every sip.

Starting with Craft Brews: Where Adirondack Ales Shine

Let me begin with craft beer, because, honestly, that's where my love affair with Adirondack beverages began. If you're even slightly into beer, the breweries here will blow your mind. I remember walking into **Lake Placid Pub & Brewery**, a cozy spot just a stone's throw from Mirror Lake. Their **Ubu Ale**—a robust English-style ale with a caramel finish—is a local legend. It's smooth but strong, with a flavor that feels like it's hugging you after a long day outdoors. I sat by the fireplace and paired it with a hearty burger, and let me tell you, it was perfection.

But the brewery scene in the Adirondacks isn't just limited to one standout. A short drive away, I found myself at **Big Slide Brewery** in Lake Placid. Their flights are the way to go if you want to sample the breadth of their creativity. Their **IPA Project Series** rotates frequently, and I tried one with subtle hints of citrus and pine—refreshing and just what I needed after exploring the trails.

For something truly off the beaten path, I ventured to **Hex and Hop Brewing** in Bloomingdale. Their name alone intrigued me, but it was the **Golden Sour Ale** that won me over. A little tangy, a little sweet, and brewed with local wild yeast, it's a drink that feels deeply connected to the land. Plus, their focus on sustainability made me appreciate each sip even more.

Adirondack Wines: A Blend of Elegance and Earthiness

If wine is more your thing, don't worry—the Adirondacks doesn't disappoint. Nestled in this wild region are small vineyards that produce wines with a rustic charm. On a whim, I visited **Adirondack Winery** in Lake George, and it was like stepping into a wine lover's dream. Their **Baco Noir**—a red wine with rich berry notes and a hint of oak—was divine. It's the kind of wine that makes you want to slow down and savor the moment, especially if you're sitting by a lake as the sun sets.

Their fruit wines, though, are the real standouts. I'm not usually a fan of sweet wines, but their **Peach Chardonnay** changed my mind. It was light, crisp, and not overly sweet—a perfect summer drink. If you go, I highly recommend doing their tasting flight. The staff is so knowledgeable and will guide you through their offerings, making the experience feel personal and fun.

Spirits with a Story: Adirondack Distilleries

I'll admit, I didn't expect to find world-class spirits in the Adirondacks, but that's exactly what I discovered. **Lake George Distilling Company** blew me away with their small-batch whiskeys. Their **Adirondack Wildfire Whiskey** has a kick of cinnamon that warms you up instantly—perfect for those chilly mountain nights. I also tried their **Bullhead Bourbon**, which was smooth, smoky, and dangerously drinkable.

Another gem is **Griffin Hill Farm Brewery**, where they make a killer **Maple Bourbon**. This one hit differently—there's something about the sweetness of the maple blending with the richness of the bourbon that feels so quintessentially Adirondack. It's like sipping the spirit of the forest, and I couldn't resist buying a bottle to take home.

For gin lovers, **Springbrook Hollow Farm Distillery** is a must-visit. Their **Adirondack High Peaks Gin** is infused with local botanicals, including juniper and wildflowers, giving it a fresh, floral profile that's unlike any gin I've had before. They also make a maple moonshine that's worth trying if you're feeling adventurous.

Non-Alcoholic Delights: Refreshing Adirondack Sips

Not every drink here is about booze—some of my favorite Adirondack beverages were non-alcoholic. Have you ever tried **maple water**? It's exactly what it sounds like: sap straight from the tree, lightly filtered and chilled. I had my first taste at a farmers' market in Saranac Lake, and it was like drinking pure mountain energy. Slightly sweet, incredibly hydrating, and full of natural electrolytes, it became my go-to refresher on hiking days.

Another standout was the herbal teas from **Mossbrook Roots Farm**. They make small-batch blends using herbs grown right in the Adirondacks. Their **Wild Forest Mint** tea was so soothing after a long day, and I even picked up a bag of their **Chamomile Lavender** blend to bring the Adirondacks home with me.

Cider: A Taste of Adirondack Apples

I can't talk about Adirondack drinks without mentioning cider. The region's crisp mountain air and fertile soil make for some incredible apple orchards, and their ciders are on another level. At **Elfs Farm Winery & Cider House**, I tried their **Adirondack Hard Cider**, which was tart, bubbly, and oh-so-refreshing. They also offer a spiced cider that's perfect for fall—it tastes like autumn in a glass.

For a more rustic vibe, I loved visiting **Ploughman's Cider**. Their **Dry-Hopped Cider** was a game-changer, with a slight bitterness from the hops that balanced the sweetness of the apples beautifully. Sitting outside with a cider in hand, surrounded by rolling hills, was one of those moments where everything feels just right.

Seasonal Specials: Adirondack Drinks with a Twist

One of the things I love about the Adirondacks is how tied to the seasons everything feels, and the drinks are no exception. In the winter, many breweries and distilleries roll out spiced and warming options. I tried a **Winter Warmer Ale** at **Raquette River Brewing,** and it had just the right amount of cinnamon and nutmeg to make me feel festive.

Spring brings unique syrups and drinks made from fresh sap. Some breweries even incorporate birch sap into their recipes, which adds a subtle, earthy sweetness. Summer is all about light, fruity beverages, like berry-infused ales or sparkling wines. And in the fall? It's cider season, hands down. There's nothing like sipping a warm spiced cider as the leaves turn brilliant shades of red and gold.

The Adirondack Drinking Culture: Laid-Back and Local

What I appreciate most about drinking in the Adirondacks is the culture around it. It's not about fancy cocktails or elaborate presentations—it's about enjoying something that's been crafted with care, often by people who live just down the road. Every sip feels personal, whether you're chatting with a brewer about their latest experiment or sampling a wine that was bottled just a few miles away.

If you ever find yourself in the Adirondacks, take the time to explore the local drinks. Trust me, it's more than just a way to quench your thirst—it's a way to connect with the land, the people, and the laid-back spirit of this beautiful region. Cheers!

Restaurants in the Adirondacks: A Culinary Adventure

The Adirondacks is not just about sprawling mountains, serene lakes, and endless outdoor adventures; it's also a treasure trove of culinary delights. Whether you're craving farm-to-table meals, hearty comfort food, or international cuisine, the Adirondacks offers a dining experience for everyone. Let me share some of my favorite restaurants in this picturesque region, where every meal comes with a side of scenic beauty.

Lake Placid Lodge Restaurant

- **Address:** 144 Lodge Way, Lake Placid, NY 12946
- **Contact:** +1 518-523-2700
- **Website:** www.lakeplacidlodge.com
- **Cuisine Type:** Fine Dining, Farm-to-Table
- **Average Meal Cost:** $40–$75
- **Opening Hours:** Daily, 6:00 PM – 10:00 PM
- **Reservations:** Highly recommended
- **Specialties:** Duck breast with blackberry jus, locally sourced trout

If you're looking for an upscale dining experience in the Adirondacks, the Lake Placid Lodge Restaurant is a must-visit. Nestled along the shores of Lake Placid, this fine dining spot boasts rustic elegance paired with a stunning view of the lake. The chef's commitment to using fresh, local ingredients shines through in every dish. I still dream about the duck breast with blackberry jus—it's the perfect balance of richness and tartness. Add a glass of wine from their carefully curated list, and you're in for an unforgettable evening.

Big Slide Brewery & Public House

- **Address:** 5686 Cascade Rd, Lake Placid, NY 12946
- **Contact:** +1 518-523-7844
- **Website:** www.bigslidebrewery.com
- **Cuisine Type:** American Gastropub
- **Average Meal Cost:** $15–$30
- **Opening Hours:** Mon–Sun, 12:00 PM – 9:00 PM
- **Reservations:** Not necessary but recommended during peak times
- **Specialties:** Beer cheese pretzels, wood-fired pizza, seasonal craft beers

For a more casual vibe, Big Slide Brewery is the place to go. I stumbled upon this gem after a long day of hiking, and it was just what I needed to recharge. Their beer cheese pretzels are addictive, and the wood-fired pizzas hit the spot. Pair your meal with one of their seasonal craft beers—I'm a fan of the IPA, but their stouts are excellent, too. The brewery's open kitchen and welcoming atmosphere make it a great spot for friends and families.

The Log House Restaurant at Garnet Hill Lodge

- **Address:** 39 Garnet Hill Rd, North River, NY 12856
- **Contact:** +1 518-251-2444
- **Website:** www.garnet-hill.com
- **Cuisine Type:** American, Farm-to-Table
- **Average Meal Cost:** $20–$50
- **Opening Hours:** Daily, 7:30 AM – 9:00 PM
- **Reservations:** Recommended
- **Specialties:** Adirondack burger, house-made soups

Perched on a hill overlooking Thirteenth Lake, the Log House Restaurant feels like a hidden retreat. The Adirondack burger, topped with local cheddar and caramelized onions, is pure comfort food perfection. But don't overlook their soups, which are made fresh daily—I had a tomato bisque here once that rivaled anything I've had in big-city restaurants. After your meal, take a stroll around the lodge; the views are just as memorable as the food.

The Dancing Bears Restaurant

- **Address:** 2404 Main St, Lake Placid, NY 12946
- **Contact:** +1 518-523-3619
- **Website:** www.highpeaksresort.com
- **Cuisine Type:** American, Comfort Food
- **Average Meal Cost:** $10–$25
- **Opening Hours:** Mon–Sun, 7:00 AM – 10:00 PM
- **Reservations:** Not necessary
- **Specialties:** Adirondack poutine, maple-glazed salmon

Located right in the heart of Lake Placid, the Dancing Bears Restaurant is a lively spot perfect for any time of day. I love starting my morning here with their hearty Adirondack poutine—a savory dish that gives you the energy to tackle any adventure. Their maple-glazed salmon is another favorite, offering a delicious nod to the region's famed syrup. The casual vibe and friendly staff make this a go-to whenever I'm in town.

Bolton Beans

- **Address:** 4963 Lake Shore Dr, Bolton Landing, NY 12814

- **Contact:** +1 518-644-3313
- **Website:** Not available
- **Cuisine Type:** Diner, American Breakfast
- **Average Meal Cost:** $10–$15
- **Opening Hours:** Daily, 7:00 AM – 2:00 PM
- **Reservations:** Walk-ins only
- **Specialties:** Pancakes, homemade corned beef hash

There's something magical about starting your day at a classic diner, and Bolton Beans is one of the best. Set in a repurposed 1940s train car, this charming spot serves up diner favorites with a local twist. The pancakes here are fluffy and golden, and the homemade corned beef hash is a must-try. On weekends, it can get busy, but the wait is always worth it.

Adirondack General Store

- **Address:** 8994 Lakeshore Dr, Hague, NY 12836
- **Contact:** +1 518-543-6161
- **Website:** www.adirondackgeneralstore.com
- **Cuisine Type:** Café, Sandwiches, Local Goods
- **Average Meal Cost:** $10–$20
- **Opening Hours:** Mon–Sat, 7:00 AM – 4:00 PM
- **Reservations:** Not necessary
- **Specialties:** Breakfast sandwiches, homemade pies

This isn't your typical restaurant—it's a cozy café and store rolled into one. The Adirondack General Store is the kind of place that feels like home. I still think about their breakfast sandwiches, piled high with eggs, cheese, and bacon on freshly baked bread. If you have a sweet tooth, don't leave without trying one of their homemade pies—the berry pie is especially delightful.

Left Bank Café

- **Address:** 36 Broadway, Saranac Lake, NY 12983
- **Contact:** +1 518-354-8166
- **Website:** www.leftbankcafesaranac.com
- **Cuisine Type:** French Bistro
- **Average Meal Cost:** $20–$40
- **Opening Hours:** Wed–Sun, 11:00 AM – 9:00 PM
- **Reservations:** Recommended
- **Specialties:** Croque monsieur, duck confit

For a taste of France in the Adirondacks, Left Bank Café is a delightful surprise. The riverside setting adds a romantic touch to any meal here. My personal favorite is the croque monsieur, with its golden, cheesy crust. On a chilly evening, the duck confit is comforting and luxurious. This café is a hidden gem, perfect for slowing down and savoring the moment.

Street Food in the Adirondacks

When you think of the Adirondacks, the mind often goes to serene lakes, towering mountains, and cozy log cabins. But what about the food? If you've ever wandered through its towns and villages, you'd know that the Adirondacks boast some of the most heartwarming street food experiences. Each bite tells a story, from local traditions to innovative twists on classics. Let me take you on a journey through the region's street food scene, with a personal touch to every spot.

Vendor: The Adirondack Pretzel Wagon

- **Location:** Main Street, Lake Placid

- **Operating Hours:** 10 AM – 8 PM
- **Specialty Dish:** Jumbo Salted Pretzels with Maple Syrup Dip
- **Average Cost:** $6
- **Must-Try:** The cinnamon-sugar pretzel with a warm, gooey caramel dip

I first stumbled upon the Adirondack Pretzel Wagon during a leisurely walk in Lake Placid. The aroma of freshly baked dough was irresistible. Their pretzels, warm and soft with just the right chew, are comfort food perfected. But what really stole my heart was the maple syrup dip—a nod to the region's love for its maple heritage. Trust me, you'll want to sit by Mirror Lake, pretzel in hand, and soak in the view.

Vendor: Timber Tacos

- **Location:** Broadway Street, Saranac Lake
- **Operating Hours:** 11 AM – 9 PM
- **Specialty Dish:** Adirondack Trout Tacos
- **Average Cost:** $9
- **Must-Try:** The smoked pulled pork taco with apple slaw

When I heard about Timber Tacos, I knew I had to visit. The idea of pairing freshly caught Adirondack trout with a zesty lime crema sounded both adventurous and local. The tacos here are a blend of bold flavors and regional pride. Each bite of the trout taco bursts with freshness, and the pork taco's smoky sweetness left me wanting more. It's the kind of place where you'll end up licking your fingers unapologetically.

Vendor: The North Country Crêpe Cart

- **Location:** Park Street, Tupper Lake
- **Operating Hours:** 8 AM – 2 PM
- **Specialty Dish:** Wild Berry Crêpes
- **Average Cost:** $8
- **Must-Try:** The Nutella and banana crêpe topped with a drizzle of local honey

Tupper Lake's mornings aren't complete without a stop at the North Country Crêpe Cart. I remember waking up to a chilly sunrise and finding solace in their wild berry crêpe. The berries, sourced locally, are a juicy explosion of flavor, perfectly complemented by a dusting of powdered sugar. The vendor's cheerful banter and the smell of crêpes on the griddle make the experience unforgettable.

Vendor: Smoky Joe's Adirondack Barbecue

- **Location:** Main Street, Old Forge
- **Operating Hours:** 12 PM – 10 PM
- **Specialty Dish:** Brisket Sliders
- **Average Cost:** $10
- **Must-Try:** The Adirondack maple-glazed ribs

Smoky Joe's is the kind of place that turns passersby into loyal fans. I still remember biting into their brisket slider—the meat was so tender it practically melted in my mouth. Pair that with their homemade smoky barbecue sauce, and you've got a match made in heaven. The ribs? Let's just say I'd gladly drive an extra hour for another serving.

Vendor: Paddler's Pizza Truck

- **Location:** Dock Street, Schroon Lake
- **Operating Hours:** 4 PM – 11 PM
- **Specialty Dish:** Adirondack Veggie Pizza
- **Average Cost:** $12 for a personal pizza
- **Must-Try:** The Adirondack Buffalo Chicken Pizza

Who would've thought you could find such incredible pizza by the lake? Paddler's Pizza Truck serves thin, crispy pies loaded with local ingredients. The veggie pizza, with its fresh tomatoes, onions, and bell peppers, is a lighter yet flavorful option. But the buffalo chicken pizza? It's a tangy, spicy masterpiece that feels like a warm hug after a day of paddling.

Vendor: Sweet Peaks Ice Cream Stand

- **Location:** Main Street, Keene Valley
- **Operating Hours:** 12 PM – 7 PM
- **Specialty Dish:** Maple Bacon Ice Cream
- **Average Cost:** $5 per scoop
- **Must-Try:** Adirondack Blueberry Cheesecake Ice Cream

I never thought ice cream could feel so tied to a place until I tasted Sweet Peaks' offerings. Their maple bacon flavor is a salty-sweet delight, but the blueberry cheesecake ice cream is what keeps me coming back. Made with local blueberries and creamy cheesecake swirls, it's like tasting summer in the Adirondacks.

Vendor: Bear Claw Doughnuts

- **Location:** Route 28, Inlet
- **Operating Hours:** 7 AM – 12 PM
- **Specialty Dish:** Adirondack Maple Cream Doughnut
- **Average Cost:** $4 per doughnut
- **Must-Try:** The chocolate-dipped doughnut with hazelnut filling

Bear Claw Doughnuts is a morning ritual for many, and I can see why. Their doughnuts are soft, fluffy, and generously filled. The maple cream doughnut, with its smooth, rich filling, pairs beautifully with a hot cup of coffee. If you're lucky enough to arrive when they're fresh out of the fryer, you're in for a treat.

Vendor: Adirondack Artisan Soup Stand

- **Location:** Farmer's Market, Glens Falls
- **Operating Hours:** 9 AM – 2 PM (Saturdays only)
- **Specialty Dish:** Wild Mushroom Soup
- **Average Cost:** $7 per bowl
- **Must-Try:** The sweet corn and potato chowder

There's something about a warm bowl of soup that feels extra special in the Adirondacks, and the Artisan Soup Stand nails it. The wild mushroom soup is earthy and comforting, while the corn and potato chowder is creamy perfection. The best part? Every ingredient is locally sourced, making every spoonful taste like a celebration of the region.

Vendor: Mountain Melt Grilled Cheese

- **Location:** Church Street, Elizabethtown
- **Operating Hours:** 11 AM – 6 PM
- **Specialty Dish:** Adirondack Cheddar and Apple Grilled Cheese
- **Average Cost:** $8
- **Must-Try:** The bacon, brie, and cranberry grilled cheese

Mountain Melt takes comfort food to a whole new level. Their Adirondack cheddar and apple grilled cheese is the perfect mix of sharp and sweet, with bread toasted to golden-brown perfection. The bacon, brie, and cranberry version? Let's just say it's worth every calorie. I dare you not to order a second sandwich.

Vendor: High Peaks Hot Dogs

- **Location:** Cascade Road, Lake Placid
- **Operating Hours:** 12 PM – 8 PM
- **Specialty Dish:** Adirondack Chili Dog
- **Average Cost:** $5
- **Must-Try:** The sauerkraut and mustard hot dog

Sometimes, nothing hits the spot like a good hot dog, and High Peaks delivers. Their chili dog is hearty and packed with flavor, but the sauerkraut and mustard combo is a classic that never disappoints. It's the kind of snack you grab before heading off for a hike, satisfying and portable.

Vendor: Adirondack Chili Shack

- **Location:** Broadway, North Creek
- **Operating Hours:** 11 AM – 7 PM
- **Specialty Dish:** Hearty Adirondack Venison Chili
- **Average Cost:** $8 per bowl
- **Must-Try:** Spicy vegetarian black bean chili

The Adirondack Chili Shack is a perfect stop on a cold day. Their venison chili is rich, flavorful, and hearty—a dish that could power you through any outdoor adventure. On my last visit, I tried the vegetarian black bean chili and was pleasantly surprised by its bold flavors and the kick of heat. They even offer cornbread on the side, which is perfect for dunking.

Vendor: The Saranac Snack Shack

- **Location:** Riverside Drive, Saranac Lake
- **Operating Hours:** 10 AM – 6 PM
- **Specialty Dish:** Adirondack Maple Bacon Burger
- **Average Cost:** $12
- **Must-Try:** Sweet potato fries with maple aioli

I can't pass through Saranac Lake without grabbing a bite from the Saranac Snack Shack. Their maple bacon burger is juicy, smoky, and slightly sweet thanks to the maple glaze on the bacon. The sweet potato fries are crispy perfection, and the maple aioli is so good you'll want to dip everything in it.

Vendor: High Mountain Waffles

- **Location:** Beach Road, Lake George

- **Operating Hours:** 8 AM – 1 PM
- **Specialty Dish:** Berry Compote and Whipped Cream Waffle
- **Average Cost:** $7
- **Must-Try:** Savory cheddar and chive waffle

High Mountain Waffles is where I go for breakfast with a view. Their sweet waffles are heavenly, especially the one topped with berry compote and whipped cream. For those who prefer savory, the cheddar and chive waffle is a game-changer. It's fluffy, cheesy, and pairs wonderfully with a side of scrambled eggs.

Vendor: Rustic Roots Coffee & Bagels

- **Location:** Market Street, Long Lake
- **Operating Hours:** 6 AM – 2 PM
- **Specialty Dish:** Everything Bagel with Maple Cream Cheese
- **Average Cost:** $5
- **Must-Try:** Cinnamon raisin bagel with Adirondack apple butter

Rustic Roots is where you start your morning when visiting Long Lake. Their everything bagel with maple cream cheese is a local favorite and perfectly balances savory and sweet. My personal pick is the cinnamon raisin bagel slathered in Adirondack apple butter—it's a comforting bite that feels like a warm hug.

Vendor: The Lakeview Lobster Roll Truck

- **Location:** Lakeshore Drive, Bolton Landing
- **Operating Hours:** 12 PM – 8 PM
- **Specialty Dish:** Adirondack Lobster Roll
- **Average Cost:** $15
- **Must-Try:** Lobster mac and cheese

Fresh lobster in the Adirondacks? You better believe it! The Lakeview Lobster Roll Truck serves up buttery, tender lobster rolls that taste like they belong on the coast. The lobster mac and cheese is decadent and creamy—a must-try for anyone who loves comfort food with a gourmet twist.

Vendor: The Adirondack Empanada Cart

- **Location:** Town Center, Ticonderoga
- **Operating Hours:** 11 AM – 7 PM
- **Specialty Dish:** Adirondack Buffalo Chicken Empanada
- **Average Cost:** $6
- **Must-Try:** Wild mushroom and Swiss empanada

Empanadas may not be what you expect in the Adirondacks, but this cart delivers! The buffalo chicken empanada is spicy, cheesy, and wrapped in a perfectly golden crust. For something earthy and unique, try the wild mushroom and Swiss empanada—it's a flavor explosion you won't forget.

Vendor: Trailside Tacos

- **Location:** Route 30, Speculator
- **Operating Hours:** 12 PM – 9 PM

- **Specialty Dish:** Adirondack Venison Taco
- **Average Cost:** $9
- **Must-Try:** Fried fish taco with cilantro lime crema

Trailside Tacos is the perfect pit stop after hiking in Speculator. Their venison taco is packed with seasoned meat and fresh toppings, while the fried fish taco is light and crispy, complemented by a tangy cilantro lime crema. Grab a spot at their outdoor seating area and enjoy your tacos with a view of the mountains.

Vendor: The Pie Wagon

- **Location:** Church Street, Keene
- **Operating Hours:** 9 AM – 5 PM
- **Specialty Dish:** Adirondack Apple Pie by the Slice
- **Average Cost:** $4 per slice
- **Must-Try:** Mixed berry crumble pie

The Pie Wagon is a dessert lover's dream. Their Adirondack apple pie is everything you want in a slice—flaky crust, perfectly spiced apples, and a touch of sweetness. The mixed berry crumble is my go-to for its tangy, juicy filling and buttery topping. Pair it with a hot cup of cider for the ultimate treat.

Vendor: Firepit Franks

- **Location:** State Route 86, Wilmington
- **Operating Hours:** 10 AM – 8 PM
- **Specialty Dish:** Campfire Chili Dog
- **Average Cost:** $6
- **Must-Try:** Adirondack cheddar cheese dog

Firepit Franks brings a campfire vibe to street food. Their chili dog is hearty and satisfying, with a smoky flavor that feels like it was cooked over an open flame. The cheddar cheese dog is a simpler option but just as tasty, thanks to the high-quality Adirondack cheddar that melts into every bite.

Vendor: Big Moose Smoothie Shack

- **Location:** Route 28, Eagle Bay
- **Operating Hours:** 9 AM – 6 PM
- **Specialty Dish:** Wild Berry Smoothie
- **Average Cost:** $6
- **Must-Try:** Adirondack Maple and Banana Smoothie

For something refreshing, head to Big Moose Smoothie Shack. Their wild berry smoothie is a burst of fruity goodness, perfect for a summer day. The maple and banana smoothie is a unique blend of flavors that highlights the Adirondack region's love for all things maple.

Vendor: Peaks Popcorn Co.

- **Location:** Main Street, Lake George
- **Operating Hours:** 10 AM – 7 PM
- **Specialty Dish:** Adirondack Maple Kettle Corn
- **Average Cost:** $5

- **Must-Try:** Cheddar and caramel popcorn mix

Peaks Popcorn Co. transforms a simple snack into a gourmet experience. The Adirondack maple kettle corn is sweet, crunchy, and completely addictive. If you're feeling adventurous, try the cheddar and caramel mix for the perfect balance of sweet and salty. It's an ideal treat to munch on while strolling by the lake.

Vendor: Cascade Crepes and Coffee

- **Location:** Cascade Road, Lake Placid
- **Operating Hours:** 8 AM – 3 PM
- **Specialty Dish:** Adirondack Maple and Walnut Crepe
- **Average Cost:** $8
- **Must-Try:** Lemon and sugar crepe

This cozy crepe stand is a breakfast or mid-morning snack haven. The maple and walnut crepe is a regional classic, with its nutty sweetness complemented by soft, buttery crepes. If you prefer a lighter option, the lemon and sugar crepe is bright, refreshing, and pairs wonderfully with their locally roasted coffee.

Vendor: Adirondack Pho Truck

- **Location:** Route 9, Chestertown
- **Operating Hours:** 11 AM – 7 PM
- **Specialty Dish:** Chicken Pho with Fresh Herbs
- **Average Cost:** $10
- **Must-Try:** Vegetarian pho with wild mushrooms

Pho in the Adirondacks? Absolutely. This food truck offers a steaming bowl of comfort with its rich, flavorful broth and fresh ingredients. The chicken pho is soothing and hearty, while the vegetarian option, with its wild mushrooms and vibrant herbs, is equally satisfying. It's a surprising yet delightful addition to the region's street food scene.

Vendor: The Ice Cream Barn

- **Location:** Route 28N, Newcomb
- **Operating Hours:** 12 PM – 9 PM
- **Specialty Dish:** Adirondack Maple Soft Serve
- **Average Cost:** $4 per cone
- **Must-Try:** Blueberry cheesecake ice cream

The Ice Cream Barn is a summer favorite, with its soft serve cones and creative seasonal flavors. The Adirondack maple soft serve is smooth, creamy, and bursting with flavor. For a special treat, try their blueberry cheesecake ice cream, which combines tangy fruit and sweet cream in every bite.

Vendor: Adirondack Potato Shack

- **Location:** Downtown, Glens Falls
- **Operating Hours:** 11 AM – 8 PM
- **Specialty Dish:** Loaded Adirondack Poutine
- **Average Cost:** $8
- **Must-Try:** Sweet potato fries with honey mustard

The Adirondack Potato Shack elevates the humble potato into something extraordinary. Their poutine, loaded with cheese curds and rich gravy, is the ultimate comfort food. The sweet potato fries, crispy and served with a tangy honey mustard dip, are a lighter but equally delicious option.

Food Markets in Adirondack: A Taste of the Local Flavors

Exploring food markets in the Adirondack region is like uncovering a treasure trove of local flavors, fresh produce, and artisanal delights. During my trips, I've often found these markets to be more than just places to shop—they're where the heart of the community beats. Let me take you through some of the best markets I've discovered in Adirondack, sharing the charm of each with you.

Saranac Lake Farmers Market

Location: Riverside Park, Saranac Lake, NY
Operating Days: Saturdays (June - October)
Operating Hours: 9:00 AM - 2:00 PM
Specialties: Farm-fresh vegetables, local honey, artisanal cheeses, handmade crafts
Average Price Range: $5–$30
Tips for Bargaining: While bargaining isn't common here, the vendors love chatting about their products, and sometimes you can score a small discount if you buy in bulk.

Nestled by the serene waters of Riverside Park, this market feels like a slice of heaven. The vibrant colors of the fresh produce always grab my attention first. I remember tasting the sweetest cherry tomatoes here, freshly picked that very morning. The friendly vendors make you feel right at home, sharing recipes and stories behind their products. Don't miss the local honey— it's infused with wildflowers from the area and makes for a delightful souvenir!

Lake Placid Farmers Market

Location: Jewtraw Park, Lake Placid, NY
Operating Days: Wednesdays (June - October)
Operating Hours: 10:00 AM - 1:00 PM
Specialties: Organic fruits, baked goods, locally brewed ciders
Average Price Range: $7–$25
Tips for Bargaining: Vendors are usually firm with prices, but engaging in a friendly conversation might lead to a bonus pastry or two!

Lake Placid's market is where I discovered my love for Adirondack-style apple cider. It was a chilly morning, and the vendor handed me a warm cup of cider that tasted like fall in a glass—crisp, tangy, and just the right amount of sweet. The baked goods here are equally irresistible, with flaky croissants and gooey cinnamon buns that seem to vanish before your eyes.

Ticonderoga Area Farmers Market

Location: Wicker Street, Ticonderoga, NY
Operating Days: Saturdays (July - September)
Operating Hours: 10:00 AM - 1:00 PM
Specialties: Freshly baked pies, handcrafted candles, Adirondack maple syrup
Average Price Range: $8–$40
Tips for Bargaining: Bring cash and ask for bundle deals— vendors appreciate regular customers and are often happy to oblige.

This quaint market is small but brimming with character. The pies here are a must-try; I once devoured a wild blueberry pie that was so rich in flavor it left me craving for more. Another gem is the locally made maple syrup. One vendor even let me sample different grades of syrup before I made my choice—it was an experience in itself!

Keene Valley Farmers Market

Location: Marcy Field, Keene Valley, NY
Operating Days: Sundays (June - October)
Operating Hours: 9:30 AM - 2:00 PM
Specialties: Organic meats, artisanal chocolates, fresh herbs
Average Price Range: $10–$50
Tips for Bargaining: Not much room for haggling, but showing interest in their craft often leads to delightful conversations and occasional discounts.

Keene Valley's market sits in the shadow of the High Peaks, offering breathtaking views alongside its delectable offerings. I still remember savoring a slice of artisanal chocolate infused with lavender here—it was unlike anything I'd ever tried. Pair that with their organic meats for a picnic, and you've got yourself a meal fit for a mountain adventure.

Adirondack Harvest Festival Market

Location: Essex County Fairgrounds, Westport, NY
Operating Days: Seasonal (September)
Operating Hours: 10:00 AM - 4:00 PM
Specialties: Local wine, gourmet jams, heirloom vegetables
Average Price Range: $12–$60
Tips for Bargaining: Vendors are usually open to bundle deals, especially near closing time.

If you're visiting during September, the Adirondack Harvest Festival is a must. I still remember the first time I stumbled upon this market—the aroma of freshly grilled corn on the cob drew me in. The local wines here are exceptional; one vendor recommended pairing their Pinot Noir with a locally made berry jam, and the combination was divine.

Glens Falls Farmers Market

Location: South Street Pavilion, Glens Falls, NY
Operating Days: Saturdays (Year-round)
Operating Hours: 8:00 AM - Noon
Specialties: Seasonal flowers, grass-fed dairy products, fresh fish
Average Price Range: $5–$35
Tips for Bargaining: While prices are fair, buying directly from the farmers can sometimes lead to small discounts.

This year-round market is my go-to for fresh fish and flowers. On one visit, I was captivated by a vibrant bouquet of sunflowers that brightened up my entire week. The dairy products are another highlight—I'm particularly fond of the creamy yogurts made from grass-fed milk.

Adirondack Farmers Market Cooperative

Location: Various locations across Adirondack towns
Operating Days: Rotating schedule (Check local listings)
Operating Hours: Typically mornings
Specialties: Adirondack cheeses, homemade soaps, craft beers
Average Price Range: $7–$50
Tips for Bargaining: Asking questions about the products often leads to generous samples or even a deal!

This cooperative brings the best of Adirondack to various towns throughout the week. I once followed their schedule across two towns and discovered a cheese vendor whose gouda was so good, I carried a wheel of it back home! Pair it with their locally brewed craft beers, and you have a perfect Adirondack evening.

Old Forge Farmers Market

Location: Park Avenue, Old Forge, NY
Operating Days: Fridays (June - October)
Operating Hours: 1:00 PM - 5:00 PM
Specialties: Adirondack crafts, fresh-cut meats, local mushrooms
Average Price Range: $10–$30
Tips for Bargaining: Vendors here are open to negotiation, especially if you're buying multiple items.

Old Forge's market has a rustic charm that makes it unforgettable. I still remember the aroma of freshly grilled sausages wafting through the air. The local mushrooms are a standout—they're earthy, flavorful, and perfect for a hearty stew.

North Creek Farmers Market

Location: Ski Bowl Park, North Creek, NY
Operating Days: Thursdays (June - September)
Operating Hours: 2:00 PM - 6:00 PM
Specialties: Locally roasted coffee, fresh herbs, organic eggs
Average Price Range: $4–$20
Tips for Bargaining: Be friendly and ask about their farming practices; vendors often reward your curiosity with discounts.

Nestled in the scenic North Creek area, this market is a favorite for its small-town charm and high-quality offerings. The locally roasted coffee is a standout—I once bought a bag of beans that filled my home with the comforting aroma of the Adirondacks. The organic eggs here are incredibly fresh, perfect for a hearty breakfast after a day of exploring the trails.

Bolton Landing Farmers Market

Location: Cross Street Parking Lot, Bolton Landing, NY
Operating Days: Fridays (June - August)
Operating Hours: 9:00 AM - 1:00 PM
Specialties: Seasonal fruits, Adirondack-made candles, gourmet chocolates
Average Price Range: $5–$30
Tips for Bargaining: If you're a regular or planning to stock up, don't hesitate to ask for a deal.

Located near Lake George, this market offers a mix of fresh produce and artisanal goods. One summer, I stumbled upon the most incredible chocolate truffles infused with local herbs— truly a treat for the senses. The vendors also sell beautifully crafted Adirondack-themed candles that make for great gifts or souvenirs.

Indian Lake Farmers Market

Location: Byron Park, Indian Lake, NY
Operating Days: Saturdays (June - September)
Operating Hours: 10:00 AM - 2:00 PM
Specialties: Adirondack maple candies, fresh baked bread, wildflower bouquets

Average Price Range: $6–$25
Tips for Bargaining: Some vendors are open to small discounts if you're purchasing several items.

Indian Lake's market is a hidden gem, where you can find the sweetest maple candies that melt in your mouth. The fresh-baked bread here is another highlight, with varieties like rosemary focaccia and sourdough that pair perfectly with any meal. I often pick up a bouquet of wildflowers—they bring the outdoors into my home.

Speculator Farmers Market

Location: Pavilion at the Speculator Ball Field, Speculator, NY
Operating Days: Thursdays (June - August)
Operating Hours: 2:00 PM - 5:30 PM
Specialties: Locally caught fish, Adirondack preserves, handmade jewelry
Average Price Range: $5–$50
Tips for Bargaining: Be polite and inquire about multiple purchases for potential deals.

Speculator's market feels like a quaint, community-driven experience. One memorable visit included sampling fresh trout that had been caught that morning—it was so good, I ended up buying enough for a small feast. The Adirondack preserves here, with flavors like blackberry and elderberry, are perfect for adding a local twist to your breakfast.

Warrensburg Farmers Market

Location: Warrensburg Mills Historic District, Warrensburg, NY
Operating Days: Fridays (May - October)
Operating Hours: 3:00 PM - 6:00 PM
Specialties: Adirondack honey, fresh greens, woodcarvings
Average Price Range: $8–$35
Tips for Bargaining: Not much bargaining here, but engaging with vendors might lead to an extra item added to your bag.

The Warrensburg Farmers Market has a nostalgic feel to it, set against the backdrop of the town's historic district. The honey here is top-notch, and one vendor even shared tips for pairing it with different cheeses. The local woodcarvings are unique and beautifully made, reflecting the Adirondack spirit.

Elizabethtown Farmers Market

Location: Court Street, Elizabethtown, NY
Operating Days: Fridays (June - September)
Operating Hours: 9:00 AM - 1:00 PM
Specialties: Fresh berries, pasture-raised meats, homemade jams
Average Price Range: $5–$30
Tips for Bargaining: Vendors sometimes offer discounts on slightly bruised fruits—still perfect for making jams or pies.

This small but mighty market is perfect for stocking up on fresh berries during the summer months. I once made an unforgettable pie using blackberries I picked up here. Their pasture-raised meats are another highlight—ideal for a grill night while enjoying the Adirondack views.

Schroon Lake Farmers Market

Location: Town Park, Schroon Lake, NY
Operating Days: Wednesdays (June - September)
Operating Hours: 10:00 AM - 2:00 PM
Specialties: Local cheeses, hand-knitted goods, fresh-cut flowers
Average Price Range: $7–$40
Tips for Bargaining: If you're interested in hand-knitted items, ask about custom orders—vendors may offer deals for repeat customers.

This market has a warm and welcoming vibe, with plenty of unique finds. The cheeses here are some of the creamiest I've tasted, and the fresh-cut flowers are perfect for brightening any space. One time, I bought a hand-knitted scarf from a local artisan—it's now a treasured part of my winter wardrobe.

Blue Mountain Lake Farmers Market

Location: Adirondack Museum Grounds, Blue Mountain Lake, NY
Operating Days: Thursdays (July - August)
Operating Hours: 10:00 AM - 3:00 PM
Specialties: Gourmet baked goods, local teas, pottery
Average Price Range: $10–$50
Tips for Bargaining: Vendors selling crafts or pottery might offer discounts if you purchase multiple items.

Located near the iconic Adirondack Experience museum, this market offers a mix of edible delights and local crafts. The gourmet baked goods are a standout—try the lemon bars, which are tangy and sweet in all the right ways. I once picked up a beautiful pottery mug here, perfect for enjoying my morning coffee.

Tupper Lake Farmers Market

Location: Municipal Park, Tupper Lake, NY
Operating Days: Thursdays (June - September)
Operating Hours: 11:00 AM - 3:00 PM
Specialties: Adirondack wine, smoked meats, fresh vegetables
Average Price Range: $8–$45
Tips for Bargaining: Chat with vendors about their products; they often appreciate your interest and might offer a deal.

Tupper Lake's market is a haven for foodies. The smoked meats here are sensational—I still dream about the smoked sausage I bought during one visit. Pair it with their Adirondack wine for an unforgettable meal. The vegetables are always fresh and full of flavor, perfect for creating a farm-to-table experience at home.

Bars and Pubs in Adirondack

When you think of the Adirondacks, you might picture serene lakes and sprawling trails, but this region also boasts a vibrant bar scene. From cozy pubs nestled in quaint towns to lively bars offering music and craft cocktails, there's something for everyone. Let me take you on a personal tour of some of the best watering holes in the Adirondacks.

The Waterhole

- **Address:** 48 Main Street, Saranac Lake, NY
- **Contact:** (518) 891-9502
- **Website:** www.saranaclakewaterhole.com
- **Specialty Drinks:** Their craft beer selection is outstanding, with a rotating list of regional brews.
- **Happy Hour:** Daily from 4 PM to 6 PM, with $2 off drafts and discounted cocktails.
- **Entertainment:** Known for hosting live bands and open mic nights, especially during their "Party on the Patio" series in the summer.
- **Opening Hours:** 3 PM to midnight (later on weekends).

This place is a gem! I stumbled upon The Waterhole one summer evening, lured by the sound of live music echoing down Main Street. Their open-air patio upstairs is the perfect spot to sip on a cold IPA while enjoying the mountain air. If you're a music lover, make sure to visit during one of their shows. It feels like the Adirondacks come alive here.

Smoke Signals

- **Address:** 2489 Main Street, Lake Placid, NY
- **Contact:** (518) 523-2271
- **Website:** www.smokesignalslny.com
- **Specialty Drinks:** Smoked Old Fashioned, made with house-infused bourbon.
- **Happy Hour:** Tuesday through Friday, 4 PM to 6 PM, featuring half-price appetizers and discounted signature cocktails.
- **Entertainment:** Occasional acoustic sets and trivia nights.
- **Opening Hours:** 11:30 AM to 10 PM.

Smoke Signals combines two of my favorite things: barbecue and craft cocktails. The bar overlooks Mirror Lake, and sipping a Smoked Old Fashioned while watching the sunset is nothing short of magical. The staff is always friendly, and if you're hungry, their brisket sliders are a must. The rustic, warm vibe makes it a great spot for a date or catching up with friends.

Big Slide Brewery & Public House

- **Address:** 5686 Cascade Road, Lake Placid, NY
- **Contact:** (518) 523-7844
- **Website:** www.bigslidebrewery.com
- **Specialty Drinks:** Their signature Big Slide IPA is a fan favorite.
- **Happy Hour:** Wednesday and Thursday from 3 PM to 5 PM, with $1 off pints and $5 appetizers.
- **Entertainment:** Beer-tasting events and occasional live music.
- **Opening Hours:** 11:30 AM to 10 PM.

I'll never forget my first visit to Big Slide Brewery. As a craft beer enthusiast, this place felt like heaven. They brew everything on-site, and you can even see the tanks from your seat. The vibe is casual, and their flight options let you sample multiple beers without overindulging. Perfect after a day on the slopes or hiking trails.

The Owl's Head Pub

- **Address:** 131 Broadway, Saranac Lake, NY
- **Contact:** (518) 891-5800
- **Website:** www.owlsheadpub.com

- **Specialty Drinks:** Adirondack Maple Mule – a twist on the classic Moscow Mule with local maple syrup.
- **Happy Hour:** Monday through Friday, 5 PM to 7 PM, with $1 off all drafts.
- **Entertainment:** Trivia nights every Thursday and karaoke on Fridays.
- **Opening Hours:** 4 PM to midnight.

This pub is as Adirondack as it gets! Cozy, friendly, and unpretentious, The Owl's Head Pub is where locals go to unwind. I've had some of the best conversations with strangers here, usually while sipping their Maple Mule. Trivia night gets competitive, but it's all in good fun.

Raquette River Brewing

- **Address:** 11 Balsam Street, Tupper Lake, NY
- **Contact:** (518) 359-3228
- **Website:** www.raquetteriverbrewing.com
- **Specialty Drinks:** Their Blue Line Blonde Ale and the seasonal Pumpkin Spice Porter.
- **Happy Hour:** Weekdays from 3 PM to 6 PM, with discounted pints and food truck specials.
- **Entertainment:** Outdoor games and weekend live music during the summer.
- **Opening Hours:** 12 PM to 9 PM.

Raquette River Brewing feels like an Adirondack backyard party. Their outdoor seating area is sprawling, with food trucks serving everything from tacos to BBQ. The beer? Absolutely top-notch. On my last visit, I couldn't get enough of their Blue Line Blonde Ale—it's light, refreshing, and pairs perfectly with a sunny afternoon.

Lake Placid Pub & Brewery

- **Address:** 813 Mirror Lake Drive, Lake Placid, NY
- **Contact:** (518) 523-3813
- **Website:** www.ubuale.com
- **Specialty Drinks:** Ubu Ale, their flagship brew, is a rich, malty English-style ale.
- **Happy Hour:** Daily from 4 PM to 6 PM, featuring $4 pints and $6 appetizers.
- **Entertainment:** Brewery tours and occasional live acoustic music.
- **Opening Hours:** 11 AM to 10 PM.

This place has history—it's been a favorite among locals and tourists for decades. Their Ubu Ale is legendary, and for good reason. I've spent many evenings here enjoying a pint on their deck, overlooking the lake. If you're into beer, their sampler is the way to go—it's like a mini adventure for your taste buds.

High Peaks Happy Hour

- **Address:** 2658 Main Street, Lake Placid, NY
- **Contact:** (518) 523-1234
- **Website:** www.highpeakshappyhour.com
- **Specialty Drinks:** Their High Peaks Margarita is a must-try.
- **Happy Hour:** Weekdays from 4 PM to 7 PM, with discounted cocktails and half-price wings.
- **Entertainment:** Pool tables, board games, and a jukebox loaded with classics.
- **Opening Hours:** 3 PM to midnight.

This is your classic "kick back and relax" kind of bar. No frills, just good vibes. I love how laid-back the atmosphere is—

perfect for unwinding after a long hike. The High Peaks Margarita is hands-down my favorite cocktail in town, and the bartenders always make you feel like family.

R.F. McDougall's Pub

- **Address:** 219 Riverside Drive, Lake Placid, NY
- **Contact:** (518) 523-2880
- **Website:** www.rfmcdougalls.com
- **Specialty Drinks:** Adirondack Whiskey Sour, made with local spirits.
- **Happy Hour:** Monday through Friday, 4 PM to 6 PM, with $2 off all drinks.
- **Entertainment:** Cozy fireplaces and live jazz on weekends.
- **Opening Hours:** 12 PM to midnight.

If you're looking for something a little more upscale but still warm and inviting, R.F. McDougall's is the spot. I visited on a snowy winter night, and their Adirondack Whiskey Sour was the perfect way to warm up. Their fireplace seating adds such a cozy touch—it's like being in a mountain lodge.

Whiteface Club & Resort Pub

- **Address:** 373 Whiteface Inn Lane, Lake Placid, NY
- **Contact:** (518) 523-2551
- **Website:** www.whitefaceclubresort.com
- **Specialty Drinks:** Adirondack Spritz with local sparkling wine and elderflower liqueur.
- **Happy Hour:** Friday and Saturday, 5 PM to 7 PM, featuring $5 cocktails and small plate specials.

- **Entertainment:** Scenic lakefront views and occasional piano music.
- **Opening Hours:** 4 PM to 10 PM.

This pub feels like a hidden retreat. After a day exploring Lake Placid, their Adirondack Spritz was a refreshing treat while sitting on the patio overlooking the lake. The upscale yet cozy atmosphere makes it perfect for special occasions or just relaxing in style.

Wunderbar & Bistro

- **Address:** 24 Cliff Avenue, Tupper Lake, NY
- **Contact:** (518) 359-2958
- **Website:** www.wunderbaradk.com
- **Specialty Drinks:** Classic German beers and homemade mulled wine in the winter.
- **Happy Hour:** Weekdays from 4 PM to 6 PM, with $1 off drafts and $6 appetizers.
- **Entertainment:** Seasonal events like Oktoberfest and live folk music.
- **Opening Hours:** 3 PM to 10 PM.

This spot blends Adirondack charm with European flair. I visited during their Oktoberfest celebration, and the mulled wine paired perfectly with the crisp autumn air. The owners are friendly, and the bar has a rustic, old-world vibe that makes you feel right at home.

The Pickled Pig

- **Address:** 2639 Main Street, Lake Placid, NY

- **Contact:** (518) 523-5777
- **Website:** www.pickledpigplacid.com
- **Specialty Drinks:** Bacon Bloody Mary, garnished with house-cured bacon.
- **Happy Hour:** Daily from 3 PM to 5 PM, featuring $5 signature cocktails and $7 sliders.
- **Entertainment:** Trivia nights on Thursdays and live acoustic music on weekends.
- **Opening Hours:** 11 AM to 10 PM.

If you love creative cocktails, The Pickled Pig is a must. Their Bacon Bloody Mary is legendary, and the smoky, savory flavor will have you ordering seconds. The laid-back vibe and friendly staff make it a fantastic spot to start or end your evening.

Northway Brewing Co. Taproom

- **Address:** 1043 US Route 9, Queensbury, NY
- **Contact:** (518) 223-0759
- **Website:** www.northwaybrewingco.com
- **Specialty Drinks:** Sunrise Session IPA, a light and fruity favorite.
- **Happy Hour:** Monday through Thursday, 4 PM to 6 PM, with discounted pints and brewery tours.
- **Entertainment:** Cornhole tournaments and occasional brewery release parties.
- **Opening Hours:** 12 PM to 9 PM.

This taproom is a haven for craft beer lovers. I spent an afternoon sampling their flights and loved the Sunrise Session IPA—it's the perfect post-hike refreshment. The relaxed atmosphere and outdoor games make it ideal for hanging out with friends.

Hot Biscuit Diner & Bar

- **Address:** 14 Park Street, Ticonderoga, NY
- **Contact:** (518) 585-3483
- **Website:** www.hotbiscuitdiner.com
- **Specialty Drinks:** Maple Bourbon Smash with local bourbon and pure Adirondack maple syrup.
- **Happy Hour:** Weekdays from 4 PM to 6 PM, with discounted draft beers and appetizers.
- **Entertainment:** Trivia nights and karaoke.
- **Opening Hours:** 7 AM to 9 PM (bar opens at 4 PM).

Don't let the diner name fool you—this spot transitions into a lively bar in the evenings. I couldn't get enough of the Maple Bourbon Smash. It's sweet, smoky, and embodies the Adirondack spirit. Pair it with their maple-glazed wings for the ultimate local experience.

Bartlett's Carry Club Tavern

- **Address:** 486 Bartlett Carry Road, Saranac Lake, NY
- **Contact:** (518) 354-5110
- **Website:** www.bartlettcarryclub.com
- **Specialty Drinks:** Adirondack Mule with local ginger beer.
- **Happy Hour:** Tuesday through Friday, 4 PM to 6 PM, featuring $1 off specialty cocktails.
- **Entertainment:** Intimate live music performances and campfire evenings.
- **Opening Hours:** 4 PM to 10 PM.

This tavern has a warm, intimate vibe that's hard to beat. I visited on a chilly fall night, and the Adirondack Mule was a perfect companion by the fire pit. It's a little off the beaten path, but worth every mile for the peace and charm it offers.

Donnelly's Ice Cream Bar

- **Address:** 155 NY-86, Saranac Lake, NY
- **Contact:** (518) 891-7747
- **Website:** www.donnellysicecream.com
- **Specialty Drinks:** Ice Cream Floats with craft beer or spiked milkshakes.
- **Happy Hour:** Saturdays from 2 PM to 5 PM, with discounts on floats.
- **Entertainment:** Retro vibes and outdoor seating with mountain views.
- **Opening Hours:** 12 PM to 8 PM.

Yes, it's an ice cream spot, but their boozy creations deserve a mention. I tried their spiked chocolate milkshake, and it was pure bliss. Donnelly's is great for a sweet twist on your typical bar outing, and their scenic location adds to the experience.

The Cottage

- **Address:** 77 Mirror Lake Drive, Lake Placid, NY
- **Contact:** (518) 302-3045
- **Website:** www.mirrorlakeinn.com
- **Specialty Drinks:** Cottage Hot Toddy with local honey and spiced whiskey.
- **Happy Hour:** Monday through Friday, 3 PM to 5 PM, featuring $6 cocktails and $8 small plates.
- **Entertainment:** Cozy fireplaces and breathtaking lake views.

- **Opening Hours:** 11 AM to 10 PM.

This charming spot by Mirror Lake is a favorite for both locals and visitors. I visited during the winter, and their Hot Toddy by the fire was just what I needed after a day in the snow. It's the kind of place that makes you want to linger, soaking in the views and warm hospitality.

Sticks & Stones Bistro and Bar

- **Address:** 739 Route 9, Schroon Lake, NY
- **Contact:** (518) 532-9663
- **Website:** www.sticksandstonesadirondack.com
- **Specialty Drinks:** Pineapple Jalapeño Margarita, a bold and spicy favorite.
- **Happy Hour:** Tuesday through Thursday, 4 PM to 6 PM, with $5 drafts and $7 specialty cocktails.
- **Entertainment:** Wood-fired pizzas and occasional live music.
- **Opening Hours:** 12 PM to 9 PM.

This place has a rustic-chic vibe and a killer cocktail menu. I couldn't resist the Pineapple Jalapeño Margarita—it's the perfect mix of sweet, spicy, and refreshing. Their wood-fired pizzas are a must, especially the Adirondack Supreme. It's a great spot for casual dining and drinks.

Nightclubs in Adirondack

The Adirondack region, known for its majestic mountains and serene lakes, might not immediately strike you as a nightlife hotspot, but it's full of surprises. Tucked away in quaint towns and bustling villages, Adirondack nightclubs offer an eclectic mix of music, energy, and camaraderie. From rustic lodges turned into lively dance spots to modern venues with booming sound systems, there's something for everyone. Let's take a dive into the club scene that keeps Adirondack alive after sundown.

The Dancing Moose Lodge

Address: 123 Mountain View Lane, Lake Placid, NY
Contact: +1 (518) 555-0123
Website: www.dancingmooselodge.com
Entry Fee: $10 cover charge
Theme Nights: "Throwback Thursdays" with 80s and 90s music
Opening Hours: Thursday-Saturday, 8 PM–2 AM
Age Restrictions: 21+

Imagine dancing under twinkling fairy lights with a view of the surrounding mountains—a unique experience offered by The Dancing Moose Lodge. This place is more than a nightclub; it's a community hub where locals and visitors come together to unwind. On my last visit, I found myself grooving to classic 90s hits on Throwback Thursday, sipping a locally brewed IPA. If you're in the mood to sing your heart out, their karaoke sessions are legendary. Pro tip: arrive early to snag a spot near the fireplace—it's a cozy touch you won't find elsewhere.

Neon Pines

Address: 78 Main Street, Saranac Lake, NY
Contact: +1 (518) 555-0456
Website: www.neonpinesclub.com
Entry Fee: $15 after 10 PM

Theme Nights: "Glow Night Saturdays" with neon body paint and EDM
Opening Hours: Friday-Saturday, 9 PM–3 AM
Age Restrictions: 18+ (ID required)

Neon Pines is the epitome of modern Adirondack nightlife. I'll admit, the first time I visited, I wasn't prepared for how vibrant this place was—glowing under blacklights with pulsating EDM beats. Glow Night Saturdays are a must; I had so much fun getting creative with neon body paint (they provide it for free!). The DJs are phenomenal, and the energy on the dance floor is infectious. If you're looking to let loose, this is your spot. Just remember to pace yourself if you're sampling their famous Neon Punch—it's potent!

Blue Ridge Beats

Address: 245 Scenic Highway, Tupper Lake, NY
Contact: +1 (518) 555-0987
Website: www.blueridgebeats.com
Entry Fee: Free before 9 PM, $10 afterward
Theme Nights: Open Mic Wednesdays and Latin Dance Fridays
Opening Hours: Wednesday-Friday, 8 PM–1 AM
Age Restrictions: 21+

For a laid-back yet lively vibe, Blue Ridge Beats hits all the right notes. Nestled in a charming log cabin-style venue, this club is all about variety. The highlight of my visit was Latin Dance Friday—it turns into a sultry salsa haven where even beginners can join in, thanks to free lessons early in the evening. On Open Mic Wednesdays, the crowd cheers for everything from acoustic ballads to spoken word poetry. It's the kind of place where strangers become friends over craft cocktails and shared love for music.

The Fire & Ice Club

Address: 332 Frozen Falls Road, Old Forge, NY
Contact: +1 (518) 555-0219
Website: www.fireandiceclub.com
Entry Fee: $20
Theme Nights: "Fire Fridays" with live fire performers
Opening Hours: Friday-Saturday, 8 PM–2 AM
Age Restrictions: 21+

If you're up for a fiery night, The Fire & Ice Club is where you need to be. I visited during their "Fire Fridays," and watching the fire performers against a snowy backdrop was surreal. Inside, the vibe is just as intense—hot beats on the dance floor and an ice bar serving up frosty cocktails. Don't skip the Firecracker Margarita; it's a crowd favorite. One tip: dress to impress but stay warm—the line to get in can be long, especially in winter.

Adirondack Groove House

Address: 55 Riverfront Drive, Glens Falls, NY
Contact: +1 (518) 555-0345
Website: www.adirondackgroove.com
Entry Fee: $12
Theme Nights: "Soul Sundays" with live jazz and blues bands
Opening Hours: Thursday-Sunday, 7 PM–12 AM
Age Restrictions: 21+

Adirondack Groove House has a unique charm—part lounge, part nightclub, all heart. I spent an unforgettable Sunday evening here soaking in live blues while sipping on a perfectly crafted Old Fashioned. The intimate setting is perfect for connecting with the music and the people around you. Thursdays are also a treat, featuring local indie bands. This spot is ideal for those who love a more relaxed, soulful vibe.

Summit Sounds

Address: 10 Summit Avenue, Bolton Landing, NY
Contact: +1 (518) 555-0678
Website: www.summitsounds.com
Entry Fee: Free for ladies on Ladies' Night; $15 for everyone else
Theme Nights: "Ladies' Night Thursdays"
Opening Hours: Thursday–Saturday, 9 PM–2 AM
Age Restrictions: 21+

Summit Sounds is a bit of a hidden gem, but once you find it, you'll keep coming back. I first visited on a whim during Ladies' Night and was blown away by the upbeat crowd and stellar DJ sets. They even have themed photo booths where you can capture the fun (props included!). The staff is incredibly friendly, and the dance floor is spacious—perfect for those who love to move. Don't leave without trying their Summit Sunset cocktail; it's as Instagram-worthy as it is delicious.

Cascade Club

Address: 88 Waterfall Way, Keene Valley, NY
Contact: +1 (518) 555-0789

Website: www.cascadeclubny.com
Entry Fee: $15
Theme Nights: "Mountain Jam Saturdays" with live rock bands
Opening Hours: Saturday, 7 PM–12 AM
Age Restrictions: 21+

For rock enthusiasts, Cascade Club is the ultimate destination. Tucked away in a scenic spot with waterfalls in the background, this club combines nature's beauty with high-energy live music. I caught a Mountain Jam Saturday show, and it felt like a private concert in the wilderness. The bands are fantastic, and the crowd is always ready to have a good time. If you're visiting, grab a spot on the balcony for the best view of the stage.

Loon Lagoon

Address: 102 Lakeshore Drive, Lake George, NY
Contact: +1 (518) 555-0321
Website: www.loonlagoonclub.com
Entry Fee: $10
Theme Nights: "Tropical Tuesdays" with tiki-themed decor and reggae music
Opening Hours: Tuesday-Saturday, 8 PM–1 AM
Age Restrictions: 21+

Loon Lagoon brings island vibes to the Adirondacks. From the moment you step in, you're transported to a tropical paradise. I couldn't resist their signature Piña Colada served in a hollowed-out pineapple—it's just as fun as it sounds! On Tropical Tuesdays, the live reggae bands create a laid-back vibe that's perfect for mingling or unwinding. Don't forget to check out their tiki photo corner for a fun souvenir of your night.

Timberline Rave

Address: 345 Alpine Street, Lake Placid, NY
Contact: +1 (518) 555-0543
Website: www.timberlinerave.com
Entry Fee: $10 before 10 PM, $20 after
Theme Nights: "Forester Fridays" featuring forest-themed décor and house music
Opening Hours: Friday-Saturday, 9 PM–2 AM
Age Restrictions: 21+

Timberline Rave is where the Adirondacks meet the underground club scene. The unique forest-themed interior—complete with faux trees and glowing mushrooms—sets the stage for a night of thumping house music. I stumbled upon this gem during a weekend trip, and it quickly became my favorite spot for its pulsating energy. The DJ lineup is always stellar, and their specialty cocktail, the "Forest Fog," adds to the whimsical vibe. Don't miss the outdoor patio—it's perfect for catching a breather under the real stars.

High Peaks Lounge

Address: 87 Summit Drive, Wilmington, NY
Contact: +1 (518) 555-0628
Website: www.highpeakslounge.com
Entry Fee: Free entry
Theme Nights: Acoustic Sundays and "Mountain Beats" Saturdays
Opening Hours: Thursday-Sunday, 7 PM–11 PM
Age Restrictions: 21+

High Peaks Lounge offers a mix of sophistication and fun, ideal for those who enjoy live music in a relaxed setting. I first visited during their Acoustic Sunday, and the vibe was perfect for winding down after a long day of hiking. Their "Mountain Beats" Saturdays feature local DJs spinning upbeat tracks, bringing a bit more energy to the crowd. Order their signature cocktail, the "Peak Punch," and enjoy the incredible views of Whiteface Mountain from the outdoor deck.

The Lakeview Underground

Address: 234 Shoreline Road, Ticonderoga, NY
Contact: +1 (518) 555-0912
Website: www.lakeviewunderground.com
Entry Fee: $5
Theme Nights: 70s Disco Nights on Fridays
Opening Hours: Friday-Saturday, 8 PM–1 AM
Age Restrictions: 18+

Hidden beneath a charming lakeside restaurant, The Lakeview Underground is a retro paradise. I had a blast during their 70s Disco Night, where the glittering disco ball and throwback beats took me back in time. The crowd was decked out in themed outfits, and I couldn't resist joining in the fun. The club's small, intimate setting makes it easy to meet new people, and their affordable drink menu ensures a good time without breaking the bank. If you're in the mood for some nostalgic fun, this is the place to be.

Snowcap Sounds

Address: 412 Winter Avenue, Lake George, NY
Contact: +1 (518) 555-0734
Website: www.snowcapsounds.com
Entry Fee: $20

Theme Nights: "Ice & Lights Fridays" with laser shows
Opening Hours: Friday-Saturday, 9 PM–2 AM
Age Restrictions: 21+

Snowcap Sounds is the ultimate spot for nightlife lovers who crave a high-tech experience. From the moment I stepped inside, I was mesmerized by the dazzling laser light shows that synchronized perfectly with the music. Their "Ice & Lights Fridays" bring a mix of electronic and pop hits, making it impossible to stay off the dance floor. The highlight for me was their frozen cocktail bar, where drinks are served in glasses made of ice—so cool, literally and figuratively!

Rocky Point Nightlife

Address: 101 Cliffside Drive, Schroon Lake, NY
Contact: +1 (518) 555-0831
Website: www.rockypointnightlife.com
Entry Fee: Free for locals, $10 for visitors
Theme Nights: Country Western Thursdays with line dancing
Opening Hours: Thursday-Saturday, 7 PM–1 AM
Age Restrictions: 18+

If you're in the mood for something different, Rocky Point Nightlife delivers. I attended their Country Western Thursday and found myself learning to line dance alongside a friendly crowd. The rustic charm of the place, complete with wagon wheel chandeliers and vintage decor, adds to the authenticity. It's a great spot to grab a cold beer, enjoy live country music, and mingle with locals who are always up for a good time.

Echo Vibes

Address: 98 Echo Lake Road, Inlet, NY
Contact: +1 (518) 555-0647
Website: www.echovibesclub.com
Entry Fee: $15
Theme Nights: "Retro Remixes Wednesdays"
Opening Hours: Wednesday-Saturday, 8 PM–1 AM
Age Restrictions: 21+

Echo Vibes is a favorite among those looking for a casual yet lively spot to dance the night away. Their "Retro Remixes" night is a blast—I couldn't resist grooving to old-school hits revamped with modern beats. The club's signature drink, the "Echo Drop," is a fruity concoction that kept me refreshed throughout the night. With its relaxed atmosphere and friendly staff, this spot quickly became one of my go-to recommendations for nightlife in the Adirondacks.

Trailhead Tavern

Address: 562 River Road, Speculator, NY
Contact: +1 (518) 555-0819
Website: www.trailheadtavern.com
Entry Fee: $5
Theme Nights: "Hiker's Happy Hour" on Thursdays with discounted drinks
Opening Hours: Thursday-Sunday, 7 PM–12 AM
Age Restrictions: 21+

Trailhead Tavern is the perfect place to celebrate a day of outdoor adventures. The rustic, wood-paneled interior gives it a cozy feel, while the DJ keeps the energy high with a mix of popular tunes. I stopped by during their "Hiker's Happy Hour," and the atmosphere was buzzing with hikers swapping trail stories over craft beers. The dance floor may be small, but the energy is infectious. For a laid-back yet spirited night, this tavern is a must-visit.

Starlight Dance Hall

Address: 150 Starlight Avenue, Indian Lake, NY
Contact: +1 (518) 555-0573
Website: www.starlightdancehall.com
Entry Fee: $12
Theme Nights: "Starlit Saturdays" with rooftop dancing
Opening Hours: Saturday, 8 PM–1 AM
Age Restrictions: 21+

For a night under the stars, Starlight Dance Hall is unbeatable. Their rooftop dance floor offers breathtaking views of the Adirondack night sky while a live DJ keeps the music going. I attended one of their "Starlit Saturdays," and the combination of fresh air, great music, and twinkling stars made for an unforgettable experience. Don't miss their "Cosmic Martini"— it's as dazzling as the view.

CHAPTER 4: TRAVEL ITINERARIES

Outdoor adventure itinerary

Exploring the Adirondacks on an outdoor adventure is nothing short of magical. From the towering peaks to the pristine lakes, every corner of this region invites you to immerse yourself in nature. I remember the first time I planned an Adirondack adventure; I was overwhelmed by the sheer number of options. To help make your journey seamless, let me take you on a three-day itinerary packed with activities, insider tips, and moments to savor.

Day 1: Arrival and Exploring Lake Placid

Morning: Kick Off with High Peaks Views

Arriving in the Adirondacks feels like stepping into a painting. Lake Placid, the crown jewel of this region, is where I love to start. After grabbing a hearty breakfast at a local favorite like **The Breakfast Club, Etc.**, I usually head to the **High Peaks Wilderness Area**. This region is famous for its 46 high peaks, and while conquering all of them is a lifetime achievement for many hikers, starting with something like **Cascade Mountain** is a perfect introduction.

The trail to Cascade is moderate and rewards you with breathtaking panoramic views. It's about 4.8 miles round-trip, so pack water, snacks, and, if you're like me, a camera for those summit selfies.

Afternoon: Paddling on Mirror Lake

After a morning hike, I like to slow things down. Mirror Lake is just steps from downtown Lake Placid, and its name says it all—it reflects the surrounding mountains so perfectly it's almost surreal. Renting a kayak or paddleboard is easy, and gliding across the glassy water is the kind of peace I didn't know I needed. If you're new to paddling, no worries—the lake is calm, and the staff at local rental shops are incredibly helpful.

Evening: Sunset and S'mores

For dinner, try **Smoke Signals** in Lake Placid. Their BBQ ribs and smoked brisket are a great way to reward yourself after an active day. But my favorite part of the evening comes later—at one of the many campsites around the area. The **Adirondack Loj Campground** is a personal favorite. Nothing beats gathering around a crackling fire under a blanket of stars, toasting marshmallows, and planning the next day's adventures.

Day 2: Conquering the Great Outdoors

Morning: A Waterfall Wonderland

Start your second day with a short drive to **High Falls Gorge**, a 30-minute detour that's absolutely worth it. It's a family-friendly spot where you can follow well-maintained trails and see some jaw-dropping waterfalls. I still remember the icy mist on my face and the roaring sound of water—it's a sensory overload in the best way.

For the more adventurous, **Ausable Chasm**, known as the "Grand Canyon of the Adirondacks," offers options like rafting, tubing, or exploring its rugged trails. I did the tubing once, and let me tell you, the thrill of bouncing along the Ausable River while surrounded by towering cliffs is something I'll never forget.

Afternoon: A Picnic by the Lake

By midday, it's time for some R&R. **Lake Champlain** is a must-visit, with plenty of picnic areas and scenic spots. I always pack a picnic lunch (local cheese, fresh bread, and fruit from a nearby market). Sitting on the shore with the lake stretching endlessly before me is one of those moments that make you stop and simply appreciate life.

If you're up for it, you can rent a bike and explore the **Lake Champlain Bikeway**, which winds through stunning landscapes. I love how the trail combines easy pedaling with moments of awe when you least expect it.

Evening: A Cozy Cabin Stay

After a full day, trade your tent for a cozy cabin or lodge for a night. Places like the **Whiteface Lodge** offer rustic luxury with warm fireplaces, hot tubs, and Adirondack-inspired decor. After soaking your tired muscles in a hot tub, you'll sleep like a baby, dreaming of the trails you've yet to explore.

Day 3: Scaling New Heights

Morning: The Thrill of Rock Climbing or Zip-Lining

If you're an adrenaline junkie like me, start your final day with rock climbing. The Adirondacks have some of the best climbing spots in the Northeast, and places like **Keene Valley** cater to both beginners and pros. With an experienced guide, even first-timers can feel the thrill of ascending a sheer rock face.

Not into climbing? No problem! The **Whiteface Mountain Adventure Zone** offers zip-lining, which is just as exhilarating. Soaring through the trees with a bird's-eye view of the forest below—it's like flying, and it's an absolute must-try.

Afternoon: Summit Whiteface Mountain

No trip to the Adirondacks feels complete without a visit to **Whiteface Mountain**. If hiking to the summit feels daunting, take the scenic **Whiteface Veterans' Memorial Highway**. Driving up, you'll feel like you're in a movie, with the winding road offering one incredible view after another. Once you reach the top, a short hike brings you to the summit for a 360-degree panorama that includes Vermont and even Canada on a clear day.

It's windy up there, so bring a jacket, but trust me—it's worth every gust.

Evening: Reflect and Relax

As the sun sets, I like to wind down at **Big Slide Brewery** in Lake Placid. Their locally crafted beer and delicious wood-fired pizzas are the perfect way to toast to an unforgettable trip. My favorite is their "Ubu Ale," named after a local legend of a dog—just one of those quirky Adirondack tales you'll love to hear.

Insider Tips for Your Adirondack Adventure

1. **Pack Smart:** Layers are key. Mornings can be crisp, but afternoons warm up quickly.
2. **Bug Spray is Your Best Friend:** The black flies and mosquitoes can be persistent, especially near water.
3. **Leave No Trace:** The Adirondacks are pristine, and keeping them that way is everyone's responsibility. Carry out whatever you carry in.
4. **Plan Ahead:** Reservations for campgrounds and popular lodges fill up fast, especially in peak season.
5. **Ask Locals:** Adirondack residents are some of the friendliest people I've met, and their tips often lead to the best-hidden gems.

A Romantic Getaway in the Adirondacks: A Storybook Adventure for Two

The Adirondacks—it's a place that feels like it was crafted by nature specifically for romance. Imagine lush forests, sparkling lakes, cozy lodges, and the kind of tranquility that makes you forget the rest of the world exists. When my partner and I decided to escape the bustle of everyday life, this magical region became our haven. Let me take you along on a romantic itinerary inspired by our unforgettable trip. Whether you're planning an anniversary, honeymoon, or just a weekend to reconnect, the Adirondacks have it all.

Day 1: Arrival and a Cozy Welcome

Midday: A Scenic Drive to the Adirondacks
The journey to the Adirondacks is part of the magic. Rolling

117

hills and charming towns accompany you as you make your way into this vast wilderness. We left mid-morning to give ourselves plenty of time to soak in the views along the way. Be sure to stop for a leisurely lunch at a roadside café; we found a little diner just outside Lake George that served the fluffiest pancakes I've ever tasted.

Afternoon: Check-In at a Romantic Lodge
Our home base for this getaway was a quaint lakeside lodge near Saranac Lake. Picture this: rustic wooden beams, a roaring fireplace, and windows that frame a serene lake like a painting. It wasn't just accommodation—it was a cocoon of comfort. Many lodges in the region offer romantic packages, complete with champagne on arrival and breakfast in bed. We opted for one of these, and I still smile thinking about the warm welcome we received.

Evening: Sunset Stroll and Candlelit Dinner
After settling in, we took a short walk along the lakefront just as the sun was setting. There's something about the way the colors dance on the water that feels like it's just for you. Dinner that night was at a small farm-to-table restaurant nearby. The ambiance—soft lighting, delicate music, and views of the lake—set the perfect tone. I still remember the richness of the duck breast I had, paired with a local pinot noir.

Day 2: Nature, Serenity, and Shared Adventures

Morning: Sunrise Kayaking on Mirror Lake
We woke up early the next day (not something I usually love to do on vacation, but this was worth it!) and headed to Mirror Lake for a sunrise kayaking session. The water was as still as glass, reflecting the fiery hues of the dawn. Paddling side by side, with only the sounds of nature around us, was both

exhilarating and grounding. It was a quiet moment where we didn't need words—just each other.

Late Morning: Breakfast at a Café in Lake Placid
Lake Placid is a cozy little town, and we found the sweetest café for breakfast. Freshly baked croissants, steaming mugs of coffee, and the hum of friendly chatter—it was the perfect way to ease into the day. From there, we explored some of the local shops, picking up handcrafted souvenirs and admiring local art.

Afternoon: Hiking Hand-in-Hand to Cascade Mountain
The Adirondacks are synonymous with hiking, and Cascade Mountain is one of the most accessible peaks for couples who want a manageable but rewarding trail. The climb took us through forests that felt straight out of a fairytale. When we reached the summit, the panoramic view of the surrounding peaks and valleys was breathtaking. We sat there for a while, sharing a thermos of hot chocolate and simply soaking in the beauty.

Evening: Private Campfire by the Lodge
Back at the lodge, the staff had set up a private campfire for us. We roasted marshmallows, shared stories, and stared at the star-filled sky. The Adirondacks have some of the darkest skies on the East Coast, making it a prime spot for stargazing. If you've never seen the Milky Way with your own eyes, this is the place to do it.

Day 3: Relaxation and Unforgettable Moments

Morning: Couples' Spa Experience
After an adventurous day, we decided to pamper ourselves with a spa session. Many lodges in the Adirondacks have on-site spas that offer couples' massages. We opted for a package that

included aromatherapy and hot stone treatments. The stress of everyday life melted away, leaving us refreshed and more connected.

Midday: Picnic by a Waterfall
For lunch, we packed a picnic and headed to High Falls Gorge. The gentle roar of the waterfall created a soothing soundtrack as we laid out our feast—a mix of artisanal cheeses, fresh bread, and local wine. It was simple, yet one of the most romantic meals I've ever had.

Afternoon: Gondola Ride at Whiteface Mountain
Later, we took a gondola ride up Whiteface Mountain. The views from the top are unparalleled—rolling green hills in summer or a winter wonderland of snow-covered peaks, depending on when you visit. Standing there together, looking out at the vast expanse, felt like being on top of the world.

Evening: A Romantic Dinner Cruise
Our final evening was spent aboard a dinner cruise on Lake George. The soft glow of the boat's lights, the lapping of the water, and live music created a dreamy atmosphere. As we dined on fresh seafood, we watched the shoreline drift by, illuminated by the golden hues of sunset.

Day 4: Farewell, with a Promise to Return

Morning: Leisurely Breakfast and a Farewell Walk
On our last morning, we lingered over breakfast, savoring the final moments of this magical getaway. Before leaving, we took one last walk by the lake. The air was crisp, and the leaves rustled gently in the breeze. We promised each other we'd return, and I have no doubt we will.

Midday: Departure, With Hearts Full
The drive back was quieter, each of us lost in thoughts of the
incredible days we'd just shared. The Adirondacks had given us
more than we could have imagined—a deeper connection,
cherished memories, and a renewed appreciation for each other.

A Coastal Itinerary Through the Adirondacks: A Journey Through Nature and Serenity

When you think of the Adirondacks, images of towering peaks,
deep forests, and serene lakes often come to mind. But let me
let you in on a secret — the Adirondacks also has a breathtaking
coastline that hugs Lake Champlain. This trip blends tranquil
lakeside retreats, charming small towns, and endless
opportunities for adventure, all with the soft whispers of the
lake's waves as your constant companion.

Let me take you on a journey — one that I've personally
cherished — along the coastal stretches of the Adirondacks.
Whether you're a seasoned explorer or a laid-back wanderer,
this itinerary offers something for everyone.

Day 1: Arrival in Essex – The Quaint Lakeside Gem

Your adventure begins in the historic town of Essex. This little
hamlet is the kind of place that makes you feel as if you've
stepped into a Norman Rockwell painting. The clapboard
houses, vintage storefronts, and a harbor bustling with activity
create a postcard-perfect vibe.

After checking into your lakeside inn — I recommend **The
Essex Inn**, a charming spot with cozy rooms and a welcoming

staff — take a leisurely stroll along Main Street. Grab a bite at **The Pink Pig**, a café serving fresh, locally sourced food. Don't miss their lemon lavender scones; they're heavenly.

Spend the evening at the **Essex Marina**. Watching the sunset over Lake Champlain is something I'll never forget. The hues of pink and orange reflecting on the calm waters set the tone for the journey ahead.

Day 2: Exploring Lake Champlain's Waters

Wake up early to the sound of gentle waves lapping at the shore. Today, the lake is calling. Rent a kayak or paddleboard from the marina. If you're like me and crave a slower start, book a morning cruise on the historic **Loch Laird**, a classic wooden boat that glides effortlessly across the lake.

As you paddle or cruise, you'll feel an overwhelming sense of peace. The vastness of Lake Champlain is humbling, but its calm demeanor is soothing. Along the way, you might spot herons fishing in the shallows or even a bald eagle soaring above.

For lunch, dock your kayak or boat at **Westport Marina**, a short journey north. Their café serves the best lobster rolls this side of the East Coast. Paired with a crisp local cider, it's the perfect lakeside meal.

Day 3: A Day in Westport – Arts and Outdoors

Westport is another gem on the Adirondack coast, and it's perfect for both art lovers and outdoor enthusiasts. Start your day at **Ballard Park**, where trails lead to scenic overlooks of the lake. The park also houses an outdoor amphitheater where concerts are often held during summer evenings.

In the afternoon, delve into the local arts scene at the **Depot Theatre**, a unique venue housed in a historic train station. Even if you're not catching a performance, the building itself is worth a visit.

I'd suggest staying at the **Westport Hotel & Tavern** for the night. They serve incredible farm-to-table dishes, and their porch dining is a lovely way to end the day.

Day 4: A Scenic Drive to Port Henry and Crown Point

The next leg of your journey takes you south along the Adirondack Coast. The drive to Port Henry is one of the most scenic routes I've ever taken. As you wind along the lake's edge, you'll pass through lush forests, open fields, and occasional glimpses of the Green Mountains of Vermont across the water.

Port Henry is a quaint, unassuming town with a rich mining history. Visit the **Iron Center Museum** to get a sense of the region's industrial past. Afterward, grab a bite at **Foote's Port Henry Diner**. Their homemade pies are the stuff of legend.

Continue to **Crown Point**, home to a stunning historic site. The **Crown Point State Historic Site** includes the ruins of two colonial forts, and the views of Lake Champlain from here are unbeatable. It's a place that combines history, nature, and serenity in perfect harmony.

Day 5: Relaxation at Lake George's Coastal End

While technically not on Lake Champlain, Lake George is close enough to be a must-add to your itinerary. Its southern shore is bustling, but the northern end offers quieter, more serene experiences. Here, I stayed at **Northern Lake George Resort**, a peaceful retreat where mornings are best spent with a cup of coffee by the water.

Spend the day exploring the lake. Rent a pontoon boat for a leisurely ride or visit **Rogers Memorial Park** in Bolton Landing for swimming and picnicking. End your day with dinner at **The Huddle Kitchen & Bar**, where the views rival the delicious dishes.

Day 6: Outdoor Adventures in Ticonderoga

Ticonderoga is the kind of place where history meets adventure. Start your morning at the iconic **Fort Ticonderoga**. Walking through the well-preserved fort, you can almost hear the echoes of past battles. The staff often dress in period attire, and the interactive exhibits make history come alive.

After your history lesson, head to **Bicentennial Park** for a relaxed hike along the La Chute River. The gentle trails are perfect for stretching your legs without overexerting yourself. For lunch, stop by **Burleigh's Luncheonette**, a retro diner with a killer club sandwich.

Day 7: Wrapping Up in Keeseville

As your journey comes to a close, head to Keeseville for a mix of natural wonders and artisan charm. The highlight here is the **Ausable Chasm**, often called the "Grand Canyon of the East." I spent hours here, hiking the trails and marveling at the waterfalls and rock formations. If you're feeling adventurous, you can even go tubing or rafting through the chasm.

Before heading home, treat yourself to a meal at **The Old Dock** in Essex. Sitting on their deck with a view of the lake, I couldn't help but reflect on how rejuvenating the past week had been.

Tips for a Perfect Coastal Adirondack Adventure

1. **Pack for variety.** The Adirondack Coast offers everything from water adventures to historic sites. Comfortable walking shoes, swimsuits, and layers for cooler evenings are essential.
2. **Plan your stays.** Accommodations in these small towns can fill up quickly, especially in peak season. Book early for the best options.
3. **Embrace the local pace.** The Adirondacks is all about slowing down and soaking in the beauty around you. Don't rush from one stop to the next; savor each moment.

Budget-Friendly Itinerary for Exploring the Adirondacks

There's something truly magical about the Adirondacks, and let me tell you, you don't need to break the bank to experience its charm. I remember planning my first trip here on a tight budget, unsure if I could make the most of it. But by the time I left, my heart (and camera roll) was full of memories, and my wallet surprisingly intact. Let me walk you through a budget-friendly itinerary that's perfect for savoring the best the Adirondacks have to offer without overspending.

Day 1: Arrival and Settling In

Afternoon: Arrival and Exploring the Base Town

Kick off your adventure by arriving at one of the Adirondack towns like Lake Placid, Saranac Lake, or Ticonderoga. I recommend checking into an affordable accommodation like a cozy hostel, budget motel, or even a well-reviewed campsite if you're up for an outdoor experience. During one of my trips, I stayed at a budget-friendly Airbnb in Saranac Lake—it felt homey and kept costs low.

Once you're settled, take some time to explore the town. Most Adirondack towns have free or low-cost attractions. For example, Lake Placid's quaint streets are dotted with Olympic history, and you can visit some spots without spending a dime, like the Olympic Speed Skating Oval. Grab a quick bite at a local deli or diner where sandwiches cost less than $10.

Evening: Sunset at Mirror Lake

As the day winds down, head to Mirror Lake in Lake Placid. It's free to walk around, and during the summer, you'll see people kayaking or paddleboarding. I once sat on the lakeside with a homemade sandwich, watching the sun dip below the mountains—it felt like I was in a postcard.

Day 2: Hiking and Waterfalls

Morning: Hike an Iconic Adirondack Trail

Hiking is the heart of the Adirondack experience, and the best part? It's free! For beginners, trails like Mount Jo near the Adirondack Loj are perfect. The parking fee is around $15, but split it with a travel buddy, and it's a steal for the views at the summit. I still remember standing atop Mount Jo, gazing at Heart Lake below and the High Peaks in the distance—it's breathtaking, and all it cost was a bit of sweat equity.

Afternoon: Visit High Falls Gorge

After a morning of hiking, treat yourself to a relatively inexpensive adventure at High Falls Gorge. Tickets cost about $10–$15, and the short walk through the gorge offers stunning views of waterfalls and rushing waters. If you're traveling with kids, this spot is a big hit—it's easy to navigate and full of photo opportunities.

For lunch, pack some snacks or a packed meal from the local grocery store. On one of my trips, I discovered that a loaf of bread, some deli meat, and a bit of mustard go a long way when you're surrounded by nature's beauty.

Evening: Campfire Vibes

If you're staying at a campsite, end your day with a cozy campfire. Pick up some marshmallows and hot dogs from a local store—it's a cheap and fun way to dine under the stars. One of my favorite Adirondack nights involved swapping stories with fellow campers and roasting s'mores until the stars lit up the sky.

Day 3: Lakes and Local Charm

Morning: Canoeing or Kayaking Adventure

The Adirondacks are famous for their pristine lakes, and renting a canoe or kayak is a budget-friendly way to soak in their beauty. Rentals typically cost $20–$40 for a few hours. I rented a kayak on Lower Saranac Lake and spent a peaceful morning paddling through glassy waters, surrounded by pine trees. If you have your own gear, even better—you can skip the rental fees!

Afternoon: Free Local Attractions

After working up an appetite, grab a bite at a local pizza joint or café. Many places offer affordable lunch specials. During my trip to Ticonderoga, I found a family-owned diner that served a hearty burger and fries for under $12.

Once fueled, explore free or low-cost attractions like Fort Ticonderoga's historic grounds. While the main fort requires an entry fee, some areas nearby are free to explore and offer fascinating insights into the region's past. Another gem? The Adirondack Experience museum in Blue Mountain Lake—it's free on certain days, so plan accordingly.

Evening: Sunset at a Scenic Overlook

Round off the day with a drive to a scenic overlook like the one on Prospect Mountain. It costs just $10 per car, and the views are priceless. Watching the sky turn pink and orange as the sun sets over the Adirondack wilderness is something I'll never forget.

Day 4: Wildlife and Farewell

Morning: Nature Walk and Wildlife Spotting

Before you head out, squeeze in a short nature walk. Trails like the Paul Smith's College VIC (Visitor Interpretive Center) are either free or ask for a small donation. Here, you can spot birds, wildflowers, and even the occasional deer. It's a peaceful way to say goodbye to the Adirondacks.

Afternoon: Local Markets and Souvenirs

On your way back, stop by a local farmers' market or roadside stand for affordable and unique souvenirs. Adirondack maple syrup and handmade crafts are budget-friendly and make great mementos. During my last visit, I picked up a small bottle of maple syrup for just $8, and every time I use it, I'm transported back to the mountains.

Budget Tips for the Adirondacks

- **Travel Off-Season:** Late spring and early fall offer fewer crowds and better prices on accommodations.

- **Cook Your Own Meals:** Grocery shopping is a lifesaver. Many budget lodgings have basic kitchens or grills.
- **Use Free Resources:** Visitor centers often have free maps and tips for no-cost activities.
- **Share Costs:** Traveling with a group? Split the cost of parking, rentals, and accommodations.
- **Stick to Nature:** With over six million acres of forest preserve, the Adirondacks have endless free outdoor adventures.

Historical itinerary for exploring the Adirondack

Visiting the Adirondacks feels like stepping into a living history book. Whether you're a history enthusiast or just curious about the stories behind this breathtaking region, there's so much to uncover. From the tales of early settlers to the rustic elegance of the Gilded Age, the Adirondack region invites you to journey back in time, and I'll guide you through a few days of exploring its historical gems.

Day 1: The Origins – Saranac Lake and Lake Placid

Morning: Discovering the Adirondack Cure

Starting in Saranac Lake, a village that became famous in the late 19th century for its tuberculosis treatment, feels like the perfect way to step into history. I recommend beginning at the **Saranac Laboratory Museum**, where you can learn about Dr. Edward Livingston Trudeau's pioneering efforts to treat tuberculosis with fresh mountain air. The museum offers a fascinating glimpse into how this small village became a haven for the sick.

Walking through the streets of Saranac Lake is like opening a time capsule. The "cure cottages," where patients once spent hours on porches soaking in the therapeutic air, are still standing. Stop by one of the many small cafés in the area for breakfast—I've had a memorable coffee and croissant at a charming little spot called **Origin Coffee Co.**.

Afternoon: The Olympic Legacy in Lake Placid

From Saranac Lake, it's just a short drive to Lake Placid, where history takes a more athletic turn. While most people think of the 1980 Winter Olympics here, the area's history stretches much further. I suggest visiting the **Lake Placid Olympic Museum** to explore artifacts from both the 1932 and 1980 Olympics. There's something magical about seeing the Miracle on Ice memorabilia in person—if you're a sports history buff like me, you'll find yourself lingering.

For lunch, the **Generations Tap & Grill** serves hearty dishes with a view of Mirror Lake. It's a great spot to relax before heading to the **John Brown Farm State Historic Site**, just a few miles outside town. John Brown, the famous abolitionist, called this area home, and his preserved farmstead gives you a powerful sense of the man and his mission.

Evening: Relax with Rustic Elegance

End your first day with a bit of Adirondack luxury. The **Lake Placid Lodge**, though modernized, maintains the rustic elegance that has defined the area since the late 1800s. Imagine sipping a locally brewed beer by the fireplace while the lake stretches out before you—it's an evening you'll remember.

Day 2: Adirondack Architecture and Gilded Age Grandeur

Morning: A Walk Through History at the Adirondack Museum

On your second day, head to Blue Mountain Lake, home to the **Adirondack Experience Museum**. This sprawling museum is an absolute treasure trove of history, detailing everything from logging and mining to the rise of the Adirondacks as a retreat for the wealthy. I once spent nearly an entire day here, marveling at the intricacies of Great Camp architecture and the ingenuity of early settlers.

Make sure to explore the outdoor exhibits, like the reproduction of a logging camp. Walking through the camp feels so authentic; it's as if the lumberjacks might come back at any moment.

Afternoon: Lunch with a View

By now, you're probably hungry, and there's no better place to enjoy lunch than on the deck of the **Prospect Point Cottages Café** overlooking Blue Mountain Lake. The view alone is worth the stop, but their sandwiches and soups are hearty and satisfying, the perfect fuel for the rest of your day.

Evening: Exploring Great Camp Sagamore

In the afternoon, make your way to **Great Camp Sagamore**, a National Historic Landmark that offers guided tours through its storied grounds. Built in the late 19th century by the Vanderbilt family, Sagamore is one of the best-preserved examples of Adirondack Great Camp architecture. Walking through its rustic, yet luxurious, rooms is like stepping into the Gilded Age.

I've stayed overnight at Sagamore during one of their weekend programs—it's an experience I'd highly recommend if your schedule allows. There's something magical about sitting by the campfire, hearing the loons call on Sagamore Lake, and imagining the grand gatherings that once took place here.

Day 3: Small Towns, Big Stories

Morning: Historic Ticonderoga

Start your day with a drive to Ticonderoga, a name that resonates with Revolutionary War history. The highlight here is **Fort Ticonderoga**, a meticulously restored fort where the past comes alive through reenactments and interactive exhibits. I was lucky enough to visit during one of their living history weekends, where costumed interpreters brought the fort's dramatic history to life.

The panoramic view from Mount Defiance, just a short drive away, is worth the detour. You can see how the fort's strategic location influenced so many battles. There's a small admission fee to drive up, but trust me, the vistas are worth it.

Afternoon: Crown Point Historic Site

From Ticonderoga, follow the scenic route along Lake Champlain to the **Crown Point Historic Site**. This is where you'll find the ruins of two forts—one French and one British—telling the story of colonial conflict in the Adirondacks. The museum on-site is small but packed with interesting artifacts, and the interpretive trails offer a peaceful way to reflect on the region's tumultuous history.

For lunch, the **Bridge Restaurant**, just near the Crown Point Bridge, serves up fresh, locally caught fish. Their fried perch sandwich is a personal favorite.

Evening: A Sunset Farewell

As your historical journey winds down, head to Westport on Lake Champlain for a quiet evening. This picturesque town feels like it hasn't changed much in a century, with its historic inns and serene waterfront. I recommend dining at **The Inn on the Library Lawn**, where you can enjoy a farm-to-table meal while the sun sets over the lake. It's a fitting end to a trip steeped in history and natural beauty.

Family-Friendly Itinerary in the Adirondacks: A Personal Adventure

When it comes to planning a family-friendly trip to the Adirondacks, let me tell you, it's like stepping into a storybook. The scenery is breathtaking, and the sheer variety of activities means there's something for everyone—whether your kids are toddlers or teens. My own family trip there felt like a much-needed escape into nature's embrace, where every day was an adventure waiting to unfold. Here's an itinerary based on our experiences, designed to create lasting memories for your family.

Day 1: Arrival and Relaxation in Lake Placid

Morning:
We kicked things off by heading to Lake Placid, a gem of a town nestled in the High Peaks region. After a scenic drive

(don't forget snacks for the little ones), we checked into a cozy family-friendly lodge. Many places in Lake Placid cater to families with kid-friendly rooms, game areas, and even pools. For us, the golden rule of travel with kids is to settle in first—let them explore their temporary "home" and get excited about the adventure.

Afternoon:
Once settled, we took a leisurely stroll around Mirror Lake. The paved path around the lake is stroller-friendly, so even if you have tiny tots in tow, it's smooth sailing. We rented a paddleboat—it was such a fun way to kick off the trip! My kids loved spotting ducks and imagining they were explorers on a grand water journey.

Evening:
Dinner was at a local spot called the Great Adirondack Brewing Company. They had a kids' menu that got the stamp of approval from my picky eaters, while my spouse and I savored some locally crafted beer and hearty comfort food. Afterward, we capped the night with a short walk under the stars—because nothing beats fresh mountain air to tire out the kids.

Day 2: Adventures in Nature

Morning:
We started the day with a hearty breakfast at our lodge, fueling up for a big adventure at the Wild Center in Tupper Lake. If there's one place you absolutely cannot miss in the Adirondacks, it's this. My kids were in awe of the interactive exhibits, especially the indoor river and the otter habitat. The real highlight, though, was the Wild Walk—a treetop trail that makes you feel like you're walking among the birds. Even I couldn't resist pretending I was a bird soaring over the forest!

Afternoon:
After a packed morning, we opted for a picnic lunch. There are plenty of spots in and around the Wild Center where you can spread out a blanket and enjoy some downtime. Pro tip: Pack snacks like trail mix and fruit to keep everyone energized without overloading on sugary treats.

Next, we headed to Bog River Falls. It's an easy, short hike (perfect for little legs), and the waterfall is absolutely stunning. We spent about an hour letting the kids splash in the shallow edges of the water—don't forget water shoes!

Evening:
Back in Lake Placid, we kept things low-key with pizza from Lisa G's, a family-friendly eatery. The relaxed vibe made it easy to unwind, and the kids were thrilled with their DIY s'mores dessert.

Day 3: High Peaks Fun and Scenic Views

Morning:
Today was all about the High Peaks. Now, don't worry—you don't have to be a seasoned hiker to enjoy them. We chose Mount Jo, a family-friendly hike with incredible views at the summit. It took us about an hour and a half round-trip. Our youngest got a piggyback ride partway up, but the older kids were ecstatic about reaching the top. The view of Heart Lake from the summit? Absolutely worth every step.

Afternoon:
For lunch, we grabbed sandwiches from a local deli and headed to the Adirondack Experience museum in Blue Mountain Lake. I wasn't sure how much my kids would enjoy a museum, but this one is so hands-on it felt like an extension of our outdoor

adventures. From learning how to paddle a canoe to exploring historic cabins, it kept everyone entertained—and even taught us a thing or two about the region's history.

Evening:
Dinner was back in Lake Placid at Generations Tap & Grill. They had plenty of kid-friendly options, and the views of the lake as the sun set made it a perfect end to the day. The kids loved the soft-serve ice cream for dessert, while my spouse and I indulged in decadent Adirondack-style cheesecake.

Day 4: Family Bonding on the Water

Morning:
No Adirondacks trip would be complete without some serious lake time. We rented a pontoon boat on Saranac Lake. This was probably one of the highlights of our trip—floating lazily on the water, stopping for a swim, and even doing a bit of fishing. Watching my kids squeal with delight as they reeled in their first tiny catches was priceless.

Afternoon:
We docked at a lakeside picnic area for lunch. Sandwiches, chips, and juice boxes never tasted so good as they did with that view. Afterward, we spent some time kayaking. My youngest sat between my legs while my oldest tackled a solo kayak for the first time—pure joy all around.

Evening:
Dinner was casual at a lakeside diner, where the kids practically inhaled burgers and fries. It was the kind of day where everyone went to bed happily exhausted, full of fresh air and good vibes.

Day 5: Farewell with a Touch of Thrill

Morning:
We spent our final morning at the Adirondack Scenic Railroad in Saranac Lake. The train ride was like stepping back in time, with beautiful views rolling past the windows. The kids were fascinated by the train itself, while we enjoyed soaking in the last bits of the Adirondacks' serene beauty.

Afternoon:
Before heading home, we made one last stop at the Ausable Chasm, known as the "Grand Canyon of the Adirondacks." If your kids love a mix of adventure and exploration, they'll adore the trails and rafting opportunities here. We chose the easier walking trails, which were just challenging enough to keep things exciting without overwhelming little ones.

Tips for a Smooth Adirondack Family Adventure

1. **Pack Layers:** Even in summer, mornings and evenings can be chilly, so bring jackets or sweaters.
2. **Snacks Are Key:** Hungry kids can quickly turn into cranky kids. Keep a stash of their favorite snacks handy.
3. **Plan Downtime:** Between hikes and activities, make sure to include quiet moments for the kids to rest.
4. **Safety First:** Always pack a first-aid kit, water bottles, and sunscreen, especially for outdoor activities.
5. **Embrace Flexibility:** Not every plan will go perfectly, but that's part of the adventure!

CHAPTER 5: CULTURAL EXPERIENCES

Festivals in Adirondack: A Vibrant Celebration of Culture, Nature, and Community

The Adirondack region of upstate New York is famous for its stunning natural beauty, rich history, and vibrant community spirit. It's no wonder that the festivals here are so deeply rooted in the culture of the area, offering visitors an opportunity to experience everything from local traditions and live music to craft markets and outdoor adventures. Let me take you on a journey through some of the most memorable festivals I've had the chance to attend in the Adirondacks. Trust me, every single one of them deserves a spot on your bucket list.

Festival: Saranac Lake Winter Carnival

Location: Downtown Saranac Lake, NY
Date: Early February
Activities: Ice palace construction, parades, fireworks, winter games, and themed activities
Tips for Visitors: Bundle up and don't miss the Torchlight Ski Parade—it's magical!

The Saranac Lake Winter Carnival is nothing short of a winter wonderland come to life. The centerpiece of this festival is the breathtaking ice palace, built every year from blocks of ice harvested directly from Lake Flower. It's a community effort, and you can feel the pride in every icy detail. I remember my first visit; the theme that year was "Outer Space," and the ice sculptures of astronauts and rockets glistened like something out of a dream under the night sky.

139

The parade, with its whimsical floats and costumed participants, is a must-see. My favorite moment? Watching kids and adults alike marvel at the fireworks display, the colors reflecting off the ice palace. If you visit, wear your warmest layers, grab a cup of hot cocoa from a local café, and find a good spot along the parade route.

Festival: Adirondack Balloon Festival

Location: Floyd Bennett Memorial Airport, Queensbury, NY
Date: Late September
Activities: Hot air balloon launches, live music, food trucks, and craft fairs
Tips for Visitors: Arrive early for the morning launches—they're worth the early wake-up call!

The Adirondack Balloon Festival is pure magic. Imagine standing in a field at sunrise, a steaming coffee in hand, watching dozens of hot air balloons inflate and slowly take to the skies. The silence is only broken by the occasional whoosh of the burners, and it feels like you're in a dream.

One year, I went up in a tethered balloon ride, and the view of the Adirondack Mountains and Lake George below took my breath away. For those who prefer to stay grounded, the craft fair and food trucks offer plenty to do. Try the maple-glazed donuts—they're unforgettable. Pro tip: bring a blanket and settle in for the evening glow, when the balloons are illuminated from within. It's pure romance under the stars.

Festival: Lake Placid Film Festival

Location: Various venues in Lake Placid, NY
Date: October
Activities: Film screenings, Q&A sessions with directors, and networking events
Tips for Visitors: Plan ahead and grab tickets for the popular films early—they sell out fast!

For movie buffs, the Lake Placid Film Festival is a hidden gem. Held in the charming Olympic village, this festival is a mix of blockbuster screenings and indie film premieres. I attended one year when a documentary about the Adirondack High Peaks was featured, and it felt so special to watch a film that celebrated the region's natural beauty right in its heart.

The Q&A sessions with filmmakers are intimate and inspiring. I'll never forget chatting with an up-and-coming director at a cozy after-party; the passion and creativity in the room were contagious. The town itself is bustling during the festival, so book accommodations early, and take some time to explore Main Street between screenings.

Festival: Tupper Lake Brew-ski

Location: James C. Frenette Sr. Recreational Trails, Tupper Lake, NY
Date: Late February
Activities: Skiing or snowshoeing to beer tasting stations along the trail
Tips for Visitors: Bring your own skis or snowshoes, and pace yourself—it's about savoring, not sprinting!

If you love craft beer and the great outdoors, the Tupper Lake Brew-ski is a must. This unique festival combines two of my favorite things: good drinks and gorgeous scenery. Participants ski or snowshoe along groomed trails, stopping at tasting stations where local breweries serve up their best ales and lagers.

I still laugh thinking about my first Brew-ski—I ended up chatting with a couple who had brought their dog along in a tiny ski harness. The atmosphere is relaxed and friendly, and the beers are top-notch. Don't worry if you're not an expert skier; the trail is beginner-friendly. Just remember to dress in layers and bring a backpack for snacks and water.

Festival: Wild Lights at The Wild Center

Location: The Wild Center, Tupper Lake, NY
Date: November to January
Activities: Illuminated forest walks, interactive light displays, and hot chocolate by the fire
Tips for Visitors: Visit on a weekday for smaller crowds and bring a camera for stunning photos.

Wild Lights transforms The Wild Center into an enchanting winter experience. The forest comes alive with artful light installations, creating an otherworldly glow that highlights the natural beauty of the Adirondacks. I brought my family last year, and watching my niece run through the glowing trees with her mittens swinging was pure joy.

The walkways are accessible and easy to navigate, making it a great option for all ages. Warm up afterward with hot chocolate or mulled cider from the café. If you can, book a spot for the behind-the-scenes tour to learn about how the light installations are designed—it's fascinating!

Festival: Adirondack Folk Festival

Location: Schroon Lake Town Park, Schroon Lake, NY
Date: August
Activities: Live folk music, artisan craft booths, storytelling, and food vendors
Tips for Visitors: Bring a lawn chair or picnic blanket and get ready to relax by the lake.

The Adirondack Folk Festival is a celebration of traditional music and community spirit. Held right on the shores of Schroon Lake, the festival feels like a step back in time. The lineup always includes talented local musicians and storytellers, and the crafts for sale are genuinely one-of-a-kind.

I once bought a hand-carved wooden bowl from a local artisan that I still use to serve snacks at dinner parties. The festival is free, but you'll want to bring some cash for the vendors and the food trucks. Grab a fresh lemonade and settle in by the water for an afternoon of toe-tapping music.

Festival: Great Adirondack Moose Festival

Location: Indian Lake, NY
Date: Late September
Activities: Moose-calling contests, guided nature hikes, and wildlife workshops
Tips for Visitors: Take part in a guided hike—it's the best way to spot wildlife!

The Great Adirondack Moose Festival is as quirky and fun as it sounds. This family-friendly event celebrates one of the region's most iconic animals: the moose. The moose-calling contest is a highlight—you haven't lived until you've heard someone attempt to mimic a moose's bellow!

Beyond the laughs, the festival also offers plenty of educational activities. I joined a guided nature hike one year, and while I didn't spot a moose, the guide's knowledge about the local ecosystem was impressive. There's also a craft fair, where you can pick up unique moose-themed souvenirs. Pack binoculars and a sense of adventure!

Festival: Ticonderoga FallFest

Location: Downtown Ticonderoga, NY
Date: Late September
Activities: Pumpkin painting, hayrides, local food vendors, live music, and a harvest market
Tips for Visitors: Arrive early for the best selection of goodies at the harvest market and bring the kids—they'll love the pumpkin painting station.

Fall in Ticonderoga is pure magic, and FallFest is the ultimate celebration of the season. I loved wandering through the streets decorated with hay bales and pumpkins while sipping warm cider. The harvest market is a treasure trove of locally made products—think jams, baked goods, and handcrafted gifts.

For families, this festival is a delight. The hayrides are a hit with kids, and the live music gives the whole event a warm, lively atmosphere. Be sure to stick around for the evening bonfire; the community gathers around to share stories and roast marshmallows.

Festival: North Creek Depot Days

Location: North Creek Railroad Depot Museum, North Creek, NY
Date: Mid-July
Activities: Historic train rides, live music, guided tours, and antique car displays
Tips for Visitors: Book your train tickets in advance—they sell out fast!

Depot Days in North Creek is a charming nod to the area's railway history. The highlight for me was the historic train ride along the Hudson River. Watching the scenery roll by while listening to stories about the Adirondacks' past made me feel like I had stepped into another era.

The museum hosts guided tours, and there's always something new to learn. If you're a fan of vintage cars, don't miss the antique car displays on the museum grounds. Pack a picnic to enjoy by the river after your ride.

Festival: Wilmington Whiteface Festival of Colors

Location: Wilmington Town Park, Wilmington, NY
Date: Early September
Activities: Craft fair, live music, food vendors, and outdoor family activities
Tips for Visitors: Take a short hike nearby to catch the fall foliage at its peak—it's spectacular!

The Festival of Colors is exactly what its name promises: a celebration of the Adirondacks' brilliant autumn hues. I've never seen a craft fair quite like this one—every booth seemed to reflect the vibrant reds, oranges, and yellows of the surrounding trees.

Families will love the festival for its laid-back vibe and kid-friendly activities, like face painting and games. My favorite moment was enjoying a homemade apple turnover while listening to a local band play folk tunes. Pro tip: Take a scenic drive up Whiteface Mountain's Veterans' Memorial Highway before or after the festival for panoramic views.

Festival: Old Forge PaddleFest

Location: Mountainman Outdoor Supply Company, Old Forge, NY
Date: May
Activities: Kayak and canoe demos, outdoor gear sales, and paddling workshops
Tips for Visitors: Wear comfortable clothes you don't mind getting wet and bring your questions—experts are on hand to help.

PaddleFest in Old Forge is the ultimate event for water lovers. Whether you're a seasoned paddler or a curious beginner, there's something for everyone. I spent an afternoon testing out kayaks on the serene waters of Old Forge Pond, guided by friendly and knowledgeable staff.

The event also features great deals on outdoor gear, so it's a fantastic time to upgrade your equipment. If you're new to paddling, the workshops offer invaluable tips and techniques. Afterward, grab lunch at a local café and enjoy the small-town charm of Old Forge.

Festival: Great Adirondack Garage Sale

Location: Various towns across the Adirondacks, including Long Lake, Tupper Lake, and Old Forge
Date: Late May
Activities: Town-wide garage sales, treasure hunting, and local food vendors
Tips for Visitors: Bring cash, a good map, and plenty of patience—there are hidden gems everywhere!

Imagine an entire region turned into a giant treasure hunt—that's the Great Adirondack Garage Sale. I spent a whole day driving from town to town, stopping at garage sales packed with everything from vintage furniture to handmade crafts.

The best part? Chatting with locals along the way and hearing their stories. It's not just about shopping; it's about connecting with the community. Pack a cooler with snacks and drinks, as you'll likely be on the road for most of the day. And don't forget to haggle—it's all part of the fun!

Festival: Blue Mountain Lake's Adirondack Lakes Center for the Arts Summer Festival

Location: Adirondack Lakes Center for the Arts, Blue Mountain Lake, NY
Date: July through August
Activities: Art exhibitions, live theater performances, music concerts, and workshops
Tips for Visitors: Check the schedule in advance and book tickets for popular performances early.

The Adirondack Lakes Center for the Arts hosts one of the most culturally rich festivals in the region. The summer I attended, I caught a performance of a locally inspired play that brought tears to my eyes—it was that powerful.

The art exhibitions are equally impressive, showcasing works from both regional and national artists. If you're feeling creative, the workshops are a fantastic way to try your hand at painting or pottery. The center is nestled in Blue Mountain Lake, so plan to spend some time exploring the area—it's postcard-perfect.

Festival: Thurman Maple Days

Location: Various sugarhouses in Thurman, NY
Date: March
Activities: Maple syrup tours, pancake breakfasts, wagon rides, and demonstrations
Tips for Visitors: Wear boots—it can get muddy—and come hungry for the pancakes!

Thurman Maple Days is a sweet celebration of spring and all things maple. Touring the sugarhouses and learning about the syrup-making process was fascinating, but the real highlight for me was the pancake breakfast. Smothered in fresh maple syrup, it was heaven on a plate.

Some sugarhouses also offer wagon rides and live demonstrations of how sap is collected and boiled. If you have a sweet tooth, stock up on maple candy and syrup to take home. Just be prepared for muddy conditions—it's all part of the experience!

Festival: Inlet's "Arts in the Park"

Location: Arrowhead Park, Inlet, NY
Date: Mid-July
Activities: Artisan booths, live music, and food vendors
Tips for Visitors: Arrive early to snag parking and the best selection of handmade goods.

Arts in the Park is a delightful showcase of Adirondack creativity. Strolling through the booths, I discovered everything from handwoven scarves to intricately carved wooden animals. One year, I even bought a beautiful landscape painting that now hangs in my living room.

The setting, right by Fourth Lake, makes the festival even more special. Grab lunch from one of the food vendors and enjoy it by the water while listening to live music. It's the perfect way to spend a summer day.

Festival: Cranberry Lake Fire and Rescue Field Day

Location: Cranberry Lake, NY
Date: July
Activities: Parades, fire truck rides, raffles, and community barbecues
Tips for Visitors: Bring a blanket for the fireworks and support the local fire department by participating in raffles.

This small-town festival is big on heart. The parade, featuring fire trucks and floats, is a nostalgic delight, and the community barbecue serves up some of the best burgers I've ever had.

The festival also includes fun activities for kids, like fire truck rides and games. The day ends with a fireworks display over

Cranberry Lake that draws the whole community together. It's a charming reminder of what makes the Adirondacks so special: its people.

Museums and Galleries in the Adirondack Region

Museum/Gallery: The Adirondack Experience: The Museum on Blue Mountain Lake

• **Address:** 9097 NY-30, Blue Mountain Lake, NY 12812
• **Contact:** +1 518-352-7311
• **Website:** www.theadkx.org
• **Opening Hours:** 10:00 AM
• **Closing Hours:** 5:00 PM (Closed in winter, seasonal hours apply)
• **Admission Fee:** $20 for adults, $12 for youth (6–17), free for children under 6
• **Special Exhibits:** Rotating seasonal exhibits focused on Adirondack heritage
• **Directions:** Located just off NY-30, look for signage pointing toward the museum. Ample parking is available onsite.
• **Recommended Visit Duration:** 3–4 hours

If you're looking for a deep dive into Adirondack history and culture, this museum is unbeatable. The sprawling campus is as much a part of the experience as the exhibits themselves, with 24 buildings spread across a stunning lakeside property. I spent nearly an entire afternoon here, drawn into everything from vintage guideboats to the tales of timber harvesting that once defined the region's economy.

One tip: Start with the indoor galleries and work your way outside. The interactive exhibits, like the ones on logging and wilderness survival, are surprisingly engaging—even for kids.

By the time you get to the outdoor replica of an Adirondack camp, you'll feel like you've stepped back in time.

Museum/Gallery: The Wild Center

- **Address:** 45 Museum Dr, Tupper Lake, NY 12986
- **Contact:** +1 518-359-7800
- **Website:** www.wildcenter.org
- **Opening Hours:** 10:00 AM
- **Closing Hours:** 5:00 PM
- **Admission Fee:** $20 for adults, $12 for youth (5–17), free for children under 5
- **Special Exhibits:** Climate Solutions exhibit and Wild Walk
- **Directions:** From Route 3, follow signs to the museum; parking is available near the entrance.
- **Recommended Visit Duration:** 3–4 hours

This place is a must for nature lovers. The Wild Center merges science with hands-on exploration, making it a favorite for families and curious adventurers alike. The standout feature for me? The **Wild Walk**, which takes you up into the treetops for a bird's-eye view of the Adirondack forest. Walking along those elevated bridges felt like stepping into a nature documentary.

Inside, the museum is packed with interactive exhibits that focus on Adirondack ecology and wildlife. I particularly enjoyed the live otter exhibit—watching them playfully swim around is oddly therapeutic. Whether you're traveling solo, as a couple, or with kids, this museum has something for everyone. Pro tip: Visit on a clear day to fully enjoy the outdoor trails.

Museum/Gallery: Saranac Laboratory Museum

• **Address:** 89 Church St, Saranac Lake, NY 12983
• **Contact:** +1 518-891-4606
• **Website:** www.historicsaranaclake.org
• **Opening Hours:** 10:00 AM
• **Closing Hours:** 4:00 PM (Closed Sundays and Mondays)
• **Admission Fee:** $7 for adults, $5 for seniors/students, free for children under 6
• **Special Exhibits:** Rotating exhibits on tuberculosis treatment in the Adirondacks
• **Directions:** In downtown Saranac Lake, walking distance from most restaurants and shops. Limited parking available.
• **Recommended Visit Duration:** 1–2 hours

This little museum is a hidden gem, especially if you're into quirky history. It tells the story of Saranac Lake's role as a hub for tuberculosis treatment in the late 19th and early 20th centuries. The old laboratory building is small but packed with fascinating artifacts, like antique medical equipment and patient journals.

When I visited, I was captivated by the personal stories of patients who came here for the fresh air cure. It's humbling and inspiring all at once. The staff here are incredibly knowledgeable—ask questions, and they'll share some intriguing anecdotes. Combine this stop with a stroll around the charming streets of Saranac Lake for a delightful afternoon.

Museum/Gallery: The Six Nations Indian Museum

• **Address:** 1466 County Route 60, Onchiota, NY 12989
• **Contact:** +1 518-891-2299
• **Website:** www.sixnationsindianmuseum.com

- **Opening Hours:** 10:00 AM
- **Closing Hours:** 5:00 PM (Seasonal, call ahead to confirm)
- **Admission Fee:** $6 for adults, $4 for seniors/children
- **Special Exhibits:** Permanent collection of Haudenosaunee artifacts
- **Directions:** Located off County Route 60, about a 20-minute drive from Saranac Lake. Watch for the museum's wooden sign.
- **Recommended Visit Duration:** 1–2 hours

Tucked away in the woods, this museum feels like a sacred space. It's entirely dedicated to the Haudenosaunee (Iroquois Confederacy), showcasing artifacts like traditional beadwork, masks, and ceremonial items. The setting itself is part of the magic—the rustic log structure is surrounded by towering pines, creating an atmosphere of reverence and respect.

I was lucky enough to visit when a Haudenosaunee elder was sharing stories. Hearing about the traditions and philosophies of the Six Nations directly from someone within the culture was unforgettable. This museum may be small, but its impact is profound. Take your time to absorb the exhibits and the tranquil setting.

Museum/Gallery: Ticonderoga Heritage Museum

- **Address:** 137 Montcalm St, Ticonderoga, NY 12883
- **Contact:** +1 518-585-2696
- **Website:** www.ticonderogaheritage.org
- **Opening Hours:** 10:00 AM
- **Closing Hours:** 4:00 PM (Seasonal, call ahead)
- **Admission Fee:** Free (donations welcome)
- **Special Exhibits:** Paper mill history and local industry displays

- **Directions:** In downtown Ticonderoga, easily accessible from Montcalm Street.
- **Recommended Visit Duration:** 1–1.5 hours

This charming museum is all about the industrial history of Ticonderoga. It's located in a former paper mill, and the exhibits do a fantastic job of bringing the town's manufacturing past to life. I especially loved the section on the iconic Ticonderoga pencils—who knew a humble pencil could have such a storied history?

The museum is small but well-organized, and the staff are passionate about preserving local heritage. If you're already in town to see Fort Ticonderoga, add this stop to your itinerary for a more well-rounded sense of the area's history.

Museum/Gallery: Fort Ticonderoga Museum

- **Address:** 102 Fort Ti Rd, Ticonderoga, NY 12883
- **Contact:** +1 518-585-2821
- **Website:** www.fortticonderoga.org
- **Opening Hours:** 9:30 AM
- **Closing Hours:** 5:00 PM (Seasonal, check website for details)
- **Admission Fee:** $27 for adults, $13 for children (5–15)
- **Special Exhibits:** Military artifacts and Revolutionary War reenactments
- **Directions:** Off NY-74, follow signs to Fort Ticonderoga. Plenty of parking available.
- **Recommended Visit Duration:** 3–4 hours

This isn't just a museum—it's a full-on historical experience. The fort itself is beautifully preserved, and the museum inside houses an impressive collection of military artifacts. I visited during one of their Revolutionary War reenactment days, which added an extra layer of excitement. Seeing actors in period costumes marching through the fort was like stepping into a time machine.

Be sure to climb up to the fort's walls for stunning views of Lake Champlain. Also, don't miss the King's Garden, a serene spot perfect for a quiet moment after the bustling exhibits.

Museum/Gallery: Lake Placid Olympic Museum

• **Address:** 2634 Main St, Lake Placid, NY 12946
• **Contact:** +1 518-302-5326
• **Website:** www.lpom.org
• **Opening Hours:** 10:00 AM
• **Closing Hours:** 5:00 PM (Hours may vary by season)
• **Admission Fee:** $10 for adults, $5 for children (6–12), free for children under 6
• **Special Exhibits:** 1932 and 1980 Winter Olympics artifacts, "Miracle on Ice" memorabilia
• **Directions:** Inside the Olympic Center, right in the heart of downtown Lake Placid. Ample parking available nearby.
• **Recommended Visit Duration:** 1–2 hours

Walking into this museum feels like stepping into a shrine of sports history. As someone who grew up watching Olympics highlights, I was thrilled to see the actual gear worn by athletes, like the skates from the legendary 1980 "Miracle on Ice" hockey game.

It's a relatively small museum, but it packs a lot of punch with its fascinating displays and interactive exhibits. If you're into winter sports or Olympic lore, this place will feel like a treasure trove. Don't forget to stop by the gift shop for quirky souvenirs—miniature gold medals, anyone?

Museum/Gallery: Adirondack History Museum

- **Address:** 7590 Court St, Elizabethtown, NY 12932
- **Contact:** +1 518-873-6466
- **Website:** www.adkhistorymuseum.org
- **Opening Hours:** 10:00 AM
- **Closing Hours:** 4:00 PM (Closed Sundays and Mondays)
- **Admission Fee:** $7 for adults, $5 for seniors/students, free for children under 6
- **Special Exhibits:** Rotating displays on Adirondack architecture and local industries
- **Directions:** Located just off Route 9, near the Elizabethtown courthouse. Parking is available nearby.
- **Recommended Visit Duration:** 1–2 hours

Nestled in a charming historic building, this museum is a delightful stop for anyone curious about the everyday lives of Adirondack residents over the years. From stories of early settlers to exhibits on the region's unique architecture, it's a comprehensive look at life in the Adirondacks.

I loved the section on Adirondack photography—it's amazing how early pioneers captured the raw beauty of these mountains. The museum also has a lovely garden area where you can relax and reflect after your visit.

Museum/Gallery: Penfield Homestead Museum

- **Address:** 703 Creek Rd, Crown Point, NY 12928
- **Contact:** +1 518-597-3804
- **Website:** www.penfieldmuseum.org
- **Opening Hours:** 10:00 AM
- **Closing Hours:** 4:00 PM (Seasonal, call ahead to confirm)
- **Admission Fee:** Donations welcome

- **Special Exhibits:** Mining and iron industry artifacts, Civil War memorabilia
- **Directions:** Off Route 22, follow Creek Road for about 2 miles. Look for the museum sign on the left.
- **Recommended Visit Duration:** 1–2 hours

Stepping into the Penfield Homestead Museum feels like entering a time capsule. This site preserves the story of Crown Point's once-thriving iron industry, complete with original tools and machinery.

One highlight for me was the restored blacksmith shop—it's fascinating to watch live demonstrations of ironworking techniques. The museum also holds Civil War artifacts, tying the local history to national events. If you're lucky, you might catch one of their annual events, like the Heritage Day celebration.

Museum/Gallery: John Brown Farm State Historic Site

- **Address:** 115 John Brown Rd, Lake Placid, NY 12946
- **Contact:** +1 518-523-3900
- **Website:** www.parks.ny.gov/historic-sites/28
- **Opening Hours:** 10:00 AM
- **Closing Hours:** 5:00 PM
- **Admission Fee:** Free (donations welcome)
- **Special Exhibits:** John Brown's abolitionist efforts, preserved 19th-century homestead
- **Directions:** Just outside Lake Placid, follow Route 73 to John Brown Road. Parking is available onsite.
- **Recommended Visit Duration:** 1–2 hours

This historic site is more than a museum—it's a pilgrimage for those interested in abolitionist history. John Brown, the fiery anti-slavery activist, spent his final days here before the infamous raid on Harpers Ferry.

Walking through his modest farmhouse was a humbling experience. The interpretive displays do an excellent job of contextualizing his fight for justice. I particularly enjoyed strolling around the surrounding grounds—it's serene, yet filled with the weight of history.

Museum/Gallery: Adirondack Art Museum at View

• **Address:** 3273 NY-28, Old Forge, NY 13420
• **Contact:** +1 315-369-6411
• **Website:** www.viewarts.org
• **Opening Hours:** 10:00 AM
• **Closing Hours:** 4:00 PM
• **Admission Fee:** $10 for adults, $5 for students, free for children under 12
• **Special Exhibits:** Rotating exhibits of Adirondack-inspired artwork
• **Directions:** Located right off Route 28 in Old Forge, next to the public library. Plenty of parking available.
• **Recommended Visit Duration:** 1–2 hours

For art enthusiasts, the Adirondack Art Museum at View is a slice of heaven. The modern building contrasts beautifully with the rugged scenery outside, and the galleries inside showcase works inspired by the Adirondacks' natural beauty.

During my visit, I was mesmerized by a photography exhibit that captured the shifting seasons of the Adirondack wilderness. The museum also hosts workshops, so if you're feeling inspired, you can try your hand at painting or pottery.

Museum/Gallery: Natural Stone Bridge and Caves Park

• **Address:** 535 Stone Bridge Rd, Pottersville, NY 12860
• **Contact:** +1 518-494-2283
• **Website:** www.stonebridgeandcaves.com
• **Opening Hours:** 9:00 AM
• **Closing Hours:** 5:00 PM
• **Admission Fee:** $18 for adults, $10 for children (5–12)
• **Special Exhibits:** Geological formations, caves, and mineral displays
• **Directions:** Off I-87, take Exit 26 and follow signs to the park.
• **Recommended Visit Duration:** 2–3 hours

Though more of a natural museum, this park is a must for geology buffs. The massive stone bridge—one of the largest marble caves in the eastern U.S.—is the star attraction. Walking through the caves, you'll find informative displays about the region's geological history.

I visited with my family, and we had a blast exploring the trails and learning about the rock formations. Kids especially love the gemstone mining activity—it's a fun and educational way to take home a unique souvenir.

Museum/Gallery: North Star Underground Railroad Museum

• **Address:** 1131 Mace Chasm Rd, Ausable Chasm, NY 12911
• **Contact:** +1 518-834-5180
• **Website:** www.northcountryundergroundrailroad.com
• **Opening Hours:** 10:00 AM
• **Closing Hours:** 4:00 PM (Closed Mondays and Tuesdays)
• **Admission Fee:** $5 for adults, free for children under 12

• **Special Exhibits:** Stories of the Underground Railroad in New York
• **Directions:** Adjacent to Ausable Chasm, follow signs to the museum entrance.
• **Recommended Visit Duration:** 1–2 hours

This museum is small but incredibly powerful. It focuses on the role of the Adirondack region in the Underground Railroad, with moving displays of personal stories and historical documents.

The curators have done an exceptional job of creating an immersive experience—I left feeling deeply inspired and more connected to the area's history. Pair this visit with a trip to nearby Ausable Chasm for a day that's both educational and adventurous.

Off-the-Beaten-Path Attractions in the Adirondacks

If you're planning a trip to the Adirondacks and want to go beyond the usual trails and tourist spots, you're in for a treat. This region is a treasure trove of hidden gems, each with its unique charm and a story waiting to be told. These off-the-beaten-path attractions may not make the front page of travel brochures, but they'll leave you with memories that last a lifetime. Here's a look at some places I've stumbled upon—places that make me smile every time I think back to those quiet, magical moments in the Adirondacks.

Tahawus Ghost Town

Location: Newcomb, NY
Why Visit: Imagine stepping back in time to a once-thriving iron mining community, now abandoned and eerily beautiful.

I'll never forget my first visit to Tahawus. It felt like uncovering a secret, wandering among the ruins of this ghost town. The crumbling structures, enveloped by moss and wildflowers, are steeped in history dating back to the 19th century. It's easy to picture the bustling life that once filled these empty spaces, with miners and their families building a community from scratch. One of the most fascinating aspects is the restored McIntyre Furnace—an imposing relic that looks like something out of a steampunk novel.

Pro tip: Go early in the morning when the mist still clings to the landscape—it adds an almost mystical quality to the experience.

Mossy Cascade Trail

Location: Near Keene Valley, NY
Why Visit: A secluded waterfall and lush greenery that feels like your own secret paradise.

I found the Mossy Cascade Trail by accident while searching for a quiet place to hike. The trail winds gently through the woods, with the sound of trickling water growing louder as you approach the falls. It's not a long hike, but the solitude and serenity are what make it special. The waterfall itself isn't grand or dramatic—it's subtle, almost shy—but that's what I love about it. It feels like nature whispering instead of shouting.

Bring a book, find a spot near the falls, and let time slip away. I once spent an entire afternoon there, listening to birds and watching the sun dapple through the trees.

Cat Mountain Fire Tower

Location: Near Cranberry Lake, NY
Why Visit: Sweeping views from a historic fire tower with no crowds.

This spot is a bit of a trek, but trust me, it's worth every step. The hike to Cat Mountain is moderate, but the payoff is extraordinary. The fire tower, perched atop the mountain, offers a 360-degree view of sprawling forests, shimmering lakes, and the distant High Peaks.

What makes it even better is the sense of accomplishment when you reach the top. Unlike the more popular fire towers in the region, you're likely to have this one all to yourself. I remember sitting up there with a thermos of coffee, watching the clouds roll by, feeling like I was on top of the world.

Rocky Peak Ridge via Giant Mountain

Location: Trailhead on Route 73, Keene, NY
Why Visit: A high-elevation ridge hike with unparalleled views and far fewer hikers than nearby trails.

Okay, I'll admit—this one's for the adventurous types. If you're up for a challenge, the hike to Rocky Peak Ridge is an absolute must. Most people stick to the Giant Mountain trail, but branching off to this ridge rewards you with jaw-dropping views and a sense of solitude that's hard to find in the Adirondacks.

The first time I hiked it, the wind was so strong at the summit that I had to crouch down to take in the views safely. But oh, what a view it was—rolling green hills, shimmering lakes, and layers of mountains stretching endlessly into the horizon. Pack plenty of water and snacks; this hike is a workout, but it's one you'll brag about for years.

The Wild Center

Location: 45 Museum Dr, Tupper Lake, NY
Why Visit: A museum-meets-nature experience, complete with treetop bridges and live otters.

While this spot might be slightly more well-known, it still flies under the radar compared to the High Peaks. The Wild Center offers a unique blend of education and adventure. My favorite part? The Wild Walk, an elevated trail that takes you through the treetops, complete with swinging bridges and a giant eagle's nest you can climb into.

On my last visit, I spent ages watching the otters—they're endlessly entertaining and seem to love putting on a show. It's a great place to bring kids, but honestly, I think adults might enjoy it even more.

John Brown Farm State Historic Site

Location: 115 John Brown Rd, Lake Placid, NY
Why Visit: A serene historical site that pays tribute to an abolitionist hero.

This isn't just a place to visit—it's a place to reflect. John Brown's farm was the final home of the famous abolitionist, and walking the grounds feels like stepping into history. The rolling fields, rustic barn, and humble farmhouse tell a story of courage and conviction.

The first time I visited, the air was crisp, and a light snow covered the ground. It was hauntingly beautiful and gave me a new appreciation for the sacrifices made by people like Brown. Whether you're a history buff or just looking for a peaceful spot, this place is worth a detour.

Split Rock Falls

Location: Off Route 9, near Elizabethtown, NY
Why Visit: A series of cascading waterfalls perfect for a summer dip.

Split Rock Falls is one of those places that locals try to keep secret—and for good reason. It's a natural swimming hole surrounded by stunning rock formations and shady trees. On a hot day, there's nothing better than wading into the cool, clear water or sitting on the rocks with your feet dangling in.

The first time I visited, I brought a picnic and ended up staying all afternoon. The sound of the falls, the laughter of other visitors, and the sheer beauty of the place made it unforgettable. Just be sure to leave no trace—this spot is as pristine as it gets.

Crown Point State Historic Site

Location: 21 Grandview Dr, Crown Point, NY
Why Visit: Historic ruins overlooking Lake Champlain.

Crown Point isn't just a scenic spot—it's a place steeped in history. The site includes the remains of two forts, one French and one British, both dating back to the 18th century. As I wandered through the ruins, I could almost hear the echoes of soldiers' footsteps and the clang of blacksmiths at work.

The views of Lake Champlain are breathtaking, especially at sunset when the sky turns shades of pink and gold. It's a quiet, contemplative place, perfect for those who want to connect with the past while soaking in the natural beauty of the Adirondacks.

Silver Lake Bog Preserve

Location: Hawkeye, NY
Why Visit: A peaceful boardwalk trail through a pristine bog.

I didn't know what to expect when I first visited Silver Lake Bog, but it quickly became one of my favorite places. The boardwalk trail takes you through a landscape that feels untouched by time—spongy moss, pitcher plants, and the occasional glimpse of wildlife.

There's a stillness here that's hard to describe but easy to feel. It's the kind of place where you can hear your own thoughts, where nature whispers its secrets to those who take the time to listen.

Blue Ledge on the Hudson

Location: Access via North River, NY
Why Visit: A dramatic cliffside view over the Hudson River, accessible by a scenic hike.

Blue Ledge is a bit of a hidden treasure that feels like it belongs in a fantasy novel. The trail takes you through dense forests before opening up to a stunning view of the Hudson River winding through the mountains.

When I visited, the fall colors were in full bloom, and the scene looked like a postcard. It's a spot that rewards those willing to go the extra mile—literally and figuratively. Pack a camera; you'll want to remember this view forever.

Poke-O-Moonshine Mountain

Location: Route 9, Chesterfield, NY
Why Visit: Stunning views from a historic fire tower and a peaceful, less-traveled trail.

Poke-O-Moonshine is one of those mountains that doesn't get the attention it deserves. The trail to the summit is a bit challenging but manageable, and the views from the top are nothing short of spectacular. What really sets this hike apart is the historic fire tower at the peak.

On my last visit, I climbed the tower and was rewarded with panoramic views of the surrounding wilderness, Lake Champlain, and even the distant Green Mountains of Vermont. It's also a great spot for birdwatching—I once saw a peregrine falcon swooping gracefully in the valley below.

Bog River Flow

Location: Tupper Lake, NY
Why Visit: A serene paddling destination surrounded by untouched wilderness.

The Bog River Flow is a paddler's dream, with calm waters that wind through lush forests and open marshlands. I rented a kayak here on a whim, and it turned out to be one of the most peaceful afternoons I've ever had.

The area is teeming with wildlife—herons, loons, and even the occasional otter. There are plenty of spots to pull over, have a picnic, and just soak in the beauty of your surroundings. The highlight for me was paddling into Lows Lake, where the sky seemed to stretch on forever, reflecting perfectly in the glassy water.

Mason Lake

Location: Off Route 30, near Speculator, NY
Why Visit: A quiet, pristine lake with stunning sunset views.

Mason Lake feels like a secret hideaway. It's easily accessible from the road, yet it remains blissfully uncrowded. The lake is small but beautiful, surrounded by towering pine trees that seem to guard its tranquility.

I discovered this spot while driving through the area and ended up staying until sunset. The colors reflected on the still water were mesmerizing. If you're lucky, you might even hear the haunting call of a loon as the day turns to dusk. Bring a blanket and some snacks—it's the perfect spot for a romantic evening or quiet reflection.

Adirondack Scenic Byway: Moose River Plains

Location: Inlet, NY to Indian Lake, NY
Why Visit: A remote drive through the heart of the wilderness with hidden trails and campsites.

The Moose River Plains is not your typical scenic byway—it's a rugged, unpaved road that takes you deep into the Adirondack wilderness. The drive itself is an adventure, with plenty of opportunities to stop and explore hidden trails, scenic viewpoints, and secluded campsites.

I once took this route during peak foliage season, and it felt like driving through a living painting. Every bend in the road revealed another breathtaking view. If you're up for a bit of solitude and a lot of natural beauty, this is the place to be.

Lost Pond

Location: Near Lake Placid, NY
Why Visit: A hidden gem for fly-fishing and peaceful hikes.

Lost Pond is one of those places that you have to intentionally seek out, but the effort is well worth it. Nestled in the woods near Lake Placid, this small, serene pond is a haven for fly-fishers and nature lovers alike.

I stumbled upon it during a hike and was struck by its stillness. The water was so clear that I could see fish swimming near the surface, and the surrounding trees reflected perfectly in the water. If you're a fan of quiet places where you can lose track of time, Lost Pond is calling your name.

Great Camp Sagamore

Location: Raquette Lake, NY
Why Visit: A historic "Great Camp" that offers guided tours and overnight stays.

Stepping into Great Camp Sagamore feels like traveling back to the Gilded Age. Built in the late 19th century as a retreat for the wealthy Vanderbilt family, this National Historic Landmark is a stunning example of rustic elegance.

I took a guided tour here, and it was fascinating to learn about the history and craftsmanship of the buildings. The surrounding forest and lake only add to the magic. If you're looking for a unique experience, you can even book an overnight stay and live like a Vanderbilt for a night.

Shelving Rock Falls

Location: Near Lake George, NY
Why Visit: A gentle hike leading to a picturesque waterfall and swimming spot.

Shelving Rock Falls is a hidden treasure that's perfect for families or anyone looking for a relaxing outdoor adventure. The hike to the falls is short and easy, but the reward is immense.

When I visited, the water was cascading down the rocks in a sparkling curtain, creating a small pool at the base where you can dip your toes or even go for a swim. It's a wonderful spot for a picnic, with plenty of shady areas to spread out a blanket and enjoy the sound of the falls.

Valcour Island

Location: Lake Champlain, near Peru, NY
Why Visit: A secluded island with hiking trails, historic ruins, and stunning lake views.

Accessible only by boat, Valcour Island feels like your own private paradise. I kayaked there with a group of friends, and it was one of the most memorable adventures I've ever had.

The island is dotted with hiking trails that lead to secluded beaches, scenic viewpoints, and even the remains of an old lighthouse. We spent the day exploring and ended it with a campfire on the shore, watching the sunset over Lake Champlain. If you're looking for an off-grid escape, this is it.

Whiteface Veterans' Memorial Highway

Location: Wilmington, NY
Why Visit: A scenic drive to the summit of Whiteface Mountain, with stops for incredible views.

While Whiteface Mountain itself is well-known, the Veterans' Memorial Highway is an underrated gem. This winding road takes you to the top, with several pull-off points where you can admire the views or take short hikes.

The summit offers a jaw-dropping panorama of the Adirondacks, but my favorite part of the experience was the journey itself. There's something magical about watching the landscape change as you ascend, with forests giving way to rocky outcroppings and sweeping vistas.

Wanakena Footbridge

Location: Wanakena, NY
Why Visit: A historic pedestrian suspension bridge over the Oswegatchie River.

The Wanakena Footbridge might not be a grand attraction, but it has a charm that's hard to resist. Spanning the Oswegatchie River, this wooden suspension bridge sways gently as you walk across, offering picturesque views of the water and surrounding forest.

I discovered it during a lazy Sunday drive and ended up spending the afternoon exploring the quaint village of Wanakena. There's a timeless quality to this place, and crossing the bridge feels like stepping into a simpler, quieter world.

Azure Mountain Fire Tower

Location: St. Regis Falls, NY
Why Visit: A short but rewarding hike to a restored fire tower with sweeping views.

Azure Mountain is one of those hikes that packs a punch despite its modest length. The trail is steep but manageable, and the view from the top is worth every bit of effort.

The fire tower has been lovingly restored, and climbing it offers an even better vantage point of the surrounding wilderness. On my last visit, I brought a thermos of hot cocoa and watched the sun dip below the horizon, painting the sky in hues of orange and pink. It was pure magic.

CHAPTER 6: PRACTICAL INFORMATION

Safety and Security Considerations

The Adirondack Mountains are a sprawling paradise of natural beauty, inviting trails, and serene lakes. Yet, like any adventure destination, navigating them safely requires preparation, awareness, and respect for the wilderness. If you're planning to explore this region, let me walk you through some essential safety and security considerations, drawn from experiences that taught me a thing or two about what it takes to enjoy the Adirondacks while staying out of trouble.

Picture this: you're surrounded by towering pines, the air is crisp, and the only sounds are birdsong and the rustling of leaves underfoot. It's easy to get swept up in the beauty of the Adirondacks, but it's also easy to forget how unpredictable nature can be. When I first ventured out on an ambitious hike through the High Peaks region, I made a rookie mistake—setting off later in the day than I should have. With sunset approaching, I realized I'd underestimated how quickly darkness falls in the dense forest. That day, I learned to always carry a reliable flashlight and backup batteries. Trust me, stumbling through shadowy trails with just a phone's flashlight isn't an experience you want to repeat.

Speaking of planning, weather in the Adirondacks can be downright capricious. One moment, the sun is beaming, and the next, dark clouds roll in with a downpour that makes you question every gear choice you made. A simple rain jacket saved me during an unexpected storm at Lake George—it's lightweight, packs easily, and can mean the difference between continuing your adventure and cutting it short. Always check the forecast, but prepare for surprises. And layers—oh, the importance of layers. It's not just about comfort; staying warm and dry can prevent hypothermia, even in the warmer months.

Navigation is another critical point. Trails in the Adirondacks are breathtaking but not always straightforward. Once, while exploring the Moose River Plains, I convinced myself I had a solid sense of direction. Spoiler alert: I didn't. After losing the trail for what felt like an eternity, I realized how much I had underestimated the importance of carrying a detailed map and compass. Now, I never venture out without both, and I've also learned to use them properly. GPS devices are fantastic but don't rely on them alone—batteries die, signals fade, and tech can fail. Analog skills are your best safety net.

Water is another factor you can't overlook. The Adirondacks are rich with lakes, rivers, and streams, and they're as tempting as they are picturesque. However, not all water is safe to drink. I made the mistake of drinking straight from a stream once, thinking, "How bad can it be?" A few days of stomach trouble answered that question loud and clear. Always carry a water filter or purification tablets. They're small, light, and lifesaving. And if you're planning to paddle or swim, be mindful of currents and cold temperatures. Some of the most beautiful lakes can be deceivingly dangerous if you're not prepared.

Wildlife is one of the Adirondacks' greatest draws, but it's also an area where you need to exercise caution. Black bears are the most notable concern, and while they're generally not aggressive, they're curious and opportunistic. During one camping trip, I learned the hard way that food storage is non-negotiable. I left a snack wrapper in my tent, thinking nothing of it, only to wake up to a bear rummaging through our campsite. Now, I religiously use bear canisters and follow the "leave no trace" principles. It's not just about protecting yourself—it's about respecting the wildlife and their habitat.

Insects, particularly ticks and mosquitoes, are another challenge. Ticks are more than just an annoyance in the Adirondacks; they can carry Lyme disease. After finding a tick on my leg post-hike, I've become religious about using insect repellent, wearing long sleeves and pants, and doing thorough tick checks at the end of the day. As for mosquitoes, they can turn a beautiful evening by the campfire into a swatting marathon. A good bug spray, preferably one with DEET, and a mosquito net for your sleeping setup are invaluable.

One of the most valuable lessons I've learned is the importance of communication. The Adirondacks can feel wonderfully remote, but that remoteness means cell service is often spotty or nonexistent. Letting someone know your plans, including your intended route and expected return time, is a must. On one trip, a simple check-in plan with a friend back home gave everyone peace of mind. And if you're really heading off-grid, consider investing in a personal locator beacon or satellite communicator. It's an expense you hope you never need, but if you do, it's worth every penny.

Let's talk about emergencies. Knowing basic first aid is an underrated but essential skill for anyone venturing into the Adirondacks. During a hike on Mount Marcy, I saw someone slip and sprain their ankle. Thankfully, they had an ace bandage and knew how to use it. Watching them handle the situation so effectively inspired me to take a first aid course. Now, I carry a well-stocked first aid kit that includes everything from adhesive bandages and antiseptic wipes to blister pads and pain relievers. You can't predict accidents, but you can prepare for them.

Fires are another thing to be cautious about. The Adirondacks have specific rules about where and when you can build campfires, and for good reason. The forest is a delicate ecosystem, and a small mistake can have catastrophic consequences. I've seen people light fires carelessly, unaware of the risk they're posing to the area and themselves. Always follow the guidelines, and when in doubt, stick to a camp stove for cooking.

Then there's the matter of group dynamics. Whether you're hiking with friends or joining a guided tour, clear communication and mutual respect can make or break your experience. On one occasion, I joined a group hike with people I didn't know well. Halfway through, differing fitness levels and expectations created tension. It was a reminder to choose your companions wisely and to discuss plans, pace, and goals before setting off. A cohesive group is not just more enjoyable—it's safer.

Lastly, mental preparation is as crucial as physical readiness. The Adirondacks can test you in ways you might not expect. There was a moment during a particularly grueling ascent when I wondered if I'd bitten off more than I could chew. But pushing through that doubt, fueled by determination and a snack (never underestimate the morale boost of a good trail mix), made reaching the summit all the sweeter. The point is, know your limits, but don't be afraid to challenge them, responsibly.

The Adirondacks are a place of wonder, adventure, and tranquility, but they demand respect. Each trip teaches me something new, whether it's about the wilderness or myself. With the right mindset, preparation, and precautions, you can explore this incredible region safely and create memories that will stay with you forever. If I've learned anything, it's that the Adirondacks don't just offer breathtaking views—they offer life lessons, too.

Money Matters and Currency Exchange

The Adirondack region holds a special charm for travelers, offering not just natural beauty and adventure but also a sense of simplicity and authenticity. When it comes to managing your money here, things can be straightforward if you know what to expect. It's a place where cash and card coexist in harmony, and while modern conveniences are available, the rustic essence of the region often means planning ahead is wise. Let me take you through my experience and the lessons I've learned along the way.

When I first visited the Adirondacks, I expected it to be like any other touristy area, with ATMs and card machines at every corner. While you'll find many places do accept cards, especially in the larger towns like Lake Placid and Saranac Lake, cash remains king in several smaller establishments. I remember stumbling upon a charming roadside diner that served the most amazing pancakes I've ever tasted. When it came time to pay, I realized they only accepted cash. Thankfully, a kind soul in the diner directed me to a nearby ATM, but the lesson stuck: always carry some cash.

Speaking of ATMs, they're not as abundant in the Adirondacks as they are in cities. Larger towns will have them, usually near banks or gas stations, but if you're venturing deeper into the wilderness or smaller communities, you may not find one for miles. Once, during a hiking trip near Tupper Lake, I ran out of cash just when I needed to pay for a parking pass at a trailhead. I had to drive back nearly 20 minutes to find an ATM. Now, I always ensure I have enough cash for parking fees, small stores, and other unexpected expenses before heading into more remote areas.

Currency exchange isn't a big concern for most travelers within the Adirondacks, as the region is within the United States, and the US dollar is the standard. However, for international visitors, it's something to consider. If you're coming from Canada, as many do, given the proximity, you might find some businesses in tourist-heavy spots accepting Canadian dollars, but the exchange rates they offer are usually not favorable. It's better to exchange your money beforehand or use a credit card with no foreign transaction fees. I remember meeting a couple from Toronto who ended up paying significantly more for a hotel room because they hadn't exchanged their currency beforehand. They laughed it off over coffee the next morning, but it was a reminder to plan ahead.

Speaking of credit cards, they're widely accepted, especially in hotels, restaurants, and retail shops in tourist hotspots. However, there are exceptions. Smaller businesses, local artisans, and some family-run attractions may prefer cash. I once bought a beautiful handcrafted wooden ornament from a local craftsman at a market in Keene Valley. He didn't accept cards, but thankfully, I had cash on hand. Moments like these make you appreciate the simplicity and personal touch of dealing directly with the creators of such unique items.

One thing that's been a game-changer for me is using mobile payment apps and services. Many businesses in the Adirondacks, especially those that cater to younger or tech-savvy travelers, now accept payment through apps like Venmo, PayPal, or Apple Pay. During a visit to a cozy café in Bolton Landing, I forgot my wallet in the car but managed to pay for my meal using my phone. It's these little conveniences that make traveling easier, even in places where you might not expect modern technology to be so readily adopted.

Budgeting for a trip to the Adirondacks is another aspect worth discussing. The cost of living in the region is generally reasonable, but like any popular destination, tourist-heavy areas can be pricier. Lodging varies widely, from budget-friendly motels to luxurious lakeside resorts. During my first trip, I stayed at a family-run bed-and-breakfast that offered a hearty breakfast included in the price—a great way to save on meals. Dining out can also range from affordable diners to upscale restaurants, so having a mix of options and planning your meals accordingly helps.

For those who enjoy outdoor activities, many of the Adirondacks' best attractions are free or require minimal fees. Hiking trails, scenic drives, and public beaches won't cost you much, but you'll need cash for things like trailhead parking or entry fees at certain state parks. I've also learned to keep small bills handy for tipping guides or staff at local establishments. It's not mandatory, but it's a kind gesture that's always appreciated.

Another tip is to be mindful of where you're withdrawing cash. Using ATMs at local banks is generally cheaper than those found in convenience stores or tourist areas, which often charge higher fees. I've been caught off guard a couple of times, paying more in ATM fees than I'd like to admit, simply because I didn't plan ahead. Now, I make it a habit to withdraw a reasonable amount of cash before entering the Adirondacks or whenever I pass through a larger town with a bank.

If you're traveling with a group or family, splitting expenses can sometimes be a hassle, but technology has made this easier too. Apps like Splitwise or even basic mobile payment services can help keep things organized. I remember a group camping trip where we pooled money for groceries, firewood, and other essentials. Using a shared expense tracker saved us from any awkward moments or confusion when it came time to settle up.

Lastly, let's talk about souvenirs and local products. The Adirondacks are known for their maple syrup, handcrafted goods, and outdoor gear. Many of these items make for great mementos or gifts, but prices can vary. I've found that shopping at local markets or directly from artisans not only gets you the best quality but also supports the local community. Once, I bought a bottle of maple syrup from a roadside stand that was far superior to anything I'd find in a supermarket, and the price was more reasonable too. Again, cash came in handy, as many of these smaller vendors don't accept cards.

In the end, managing money in the Adirondacks is about balance and preparation. Carrying a mix of cash and cards, planning for occasional fees, and being aware of where and how you spend can make your trip smoother and more enjoyable. It's a region that invites you to slow down and embrace a simpler way of life, and that includes how you handle your finances. By being mindful and adaptable, you'll be free to focus on the breathtaking scenery, warm hospitality, and unforgettable experiences that make the Adirondacks truly special.

Health Precautions

Visiting the Adirondacks is like stepping into nature's most beautiful embrace. The region's charm lies in its pristine lakes, towering peaks, and dense forests, all begging to be explored. However, just as every adventure requires a little preparation, so does a journey into the wilds of this incredible landscape. Health and safety might not be the first thing on your mind when planning your trip, but trust me—being prepared makes all the difference in ensuring your experience is memorable for all the right reasons.

The first thing that comes to mind when I think of the Adirondacks is its endless trails. They're breathtaking, no doubt, but hiking here isn't just a casual stroll in the park. You'll want to be physically ready for it. The terrain can be demanding, with rocky paths and steep inclines. I learned this the hard way on my first hike. A few miles in, my legs were burning, and I was gulping down water faster than I should have. That's when I realized the importance of pacing myself and staying hydrated—not just when I felt thirsty but consistently throughout the day. And let me tell you, carrying enough water is crucial. You might think there are plenty of streams around, but drinking untreated water isn't worth the risk of catching something like giardia.

Speaking of hydration, let's talk about food. You'll burn more energy than you realize while hiking, especially if you're tackling some of the higher peaks like Mount Marcy. Packing snacks like nuts, energy bars, and dried fruits is a lifesaver. They're lightweight and give you the boost you need when you're halfway up a mountain and starting to question your life choices. Don't forget to plan your meals if you're camping overnight. A little extra effort in packing high-energy, lightweight foods can make all the difference.

Now, as much as I love the idea of being one with nature, it's not all sunshine and rainbows out there. Bugs can be relentless, especially in the warmer months. Mosquitoes and black flies are practically the unofficial mascots of the Adirondacks in spring and early summer. Trust me when I say you'll want a good insect repellent—something with DEET or picaridin works wonders. And don't forget to check yourself for ticks. Lyme disease is a real concern in this area, and those little critters can latch on without you even noticing. I've made it a habit to do a full-body check at the end of every day, especially after walking through tall grass or bushy trails.

Weather in the Adirondacks can be unpredictable. One minute, it's sunny and warm; the next, you're caught in a sudden downpour. I've been caught in more surprise rainstorms than I care to admit, and the key is always being prepared. Dressing in layers and carrying a waterproof jacket is a game-changer. You can peel layers off when it gets warm and bundle up if the temperature drops. And don't underestimate the importance of good hiking boots. Your feet will thank you after a day of trekking over rocks and roots. I've seen people try to hike in sneakers, and let's just say they weren't smiling by the end of the trail.

Another thing I didn't fully appreciate until I experienced it was the intensity of the sun, especially when you're out on a lake or hiking above the treeline. Sunburns happen faster than you'd think, even on cloudy days. Sunscreen is non-negotiable, and a wide-brimmed hat is your best friend. Sunglasses are another must, particularly if you're paddling on one of the many lakes. The glare off the water can be brutal.

Speaking of lakes, the water might look inviting, but it's not always as warm as it seems. Even in summer, some lakes and streams are cold enough to take your breath away. If you're planning to swim, ease in gradually to avoid shocking your system. And always be mindful of your surroundings. Not all areas are safe for swimming, and currents can be deceiving. I remember one time when a friend and I decided to cool off in a seemingly calm lake, only to find ourselves fighting a surprisingly strong current. It was a wake-up call to always prioritize safety over spontaneity.

For those planning to camp, let's talk about hygiene. Being in the wilderness doesn't mean you have to forgo cleanliness. Bringing biodegradable soap and using it sparingly helps minimize your impact on the environment while keeping you fresh. And let's not forget about hand sanitizer—it's a small thing that goes a long way, especially before meals. Another tip? Pack a first aid kit. You don't need to go overboard, but having essentials like band-aids, antiseptic wipes, and pain relievers can save the day. I've had my fair share of blisters and scrapes, and being able to patch myself up on the go is invaluable.

Wildlife is another aspect of the Adirondacks that demands respect. Bears are a part of life here, and while encounters are rare, they're not impossible. Proper food storage is critical. Most campsites require you to use bear canisters, which keep your food safe and prevent bears from associating humans with meals. I learned to hang my food bag well away from my campsite before I started using a bear canister—it's an art form, let me tell you. And no matter how tempting it is, never feed wildlife. It's bad for them and potentially dangerous for you.

Let's not forget the importance of knowing your limits. It's easy to get caught up in the excitement of bagging peaks or exploring remote areas, but pushing yourself too hard can lead to exhaustion or worse. I've learned to listen to my body and adjust my plans if needed. Sometimes, it's better to enjoy a shorter hike or take an extra rest day rather than risk injury or burnout.

Cell service can be spotty in many parts of the Adirondacks, so letting someone know your plans before heading out is essential. I always share my itinerary with a friend or family member, including where I plan to go and when I expect to be back. It's a simple precaution that can make all the difference if something goes wrong.

Finally, don't forget to savor the moment. The Adirondacks have a way of grounding you, reminding you of the beauty and power of nature. It's easy to get caught up in logistics and precautions, but take time to soak it all in. The crisp morning air, the sound of leaves rustling in the wind, and the feeling of cool water on a hot day—it's all part of the magic. Staying healthy and prepared just ensures you can fully enjoy every second of it.

So, as you pack your bags and plan your itinerary, keep these tips in mind. The Adirondacks are a wonderland waiting to be explored, and with a little preparation, you'll be able to immerse yourself in its beauty without a care in the world. Safe travels and happy adventuring!

Emergency Contact Numbers in the Adirondacks: What You Need to Know

When venturing into the Adirondacks, it's easy to get swept away by the beauty of the towering peaks, the serenity of its lakes, and the whispering forests. But as someone who has spent years exploring this incredible region, I can tell you that preparedness is key. Having a list of emergency contact numbers and knowing when and how to use them can make all the difference. Let me walk you through some essential information so that you can enjoy your trip with confidence.

The Adirondacks, with their vast wilderness and rural communities, are breathtaking but also isolated in some areas. Cellular service can be spotty, and depending on where you're hiking, camping, or exploring, help may not be immediately accessible. I've learned this the hard way, but having these emergency numbers handy can save precious time in situations where every second counts.

Adirondack Park Agency: Your Go-To for Park-Related Issues

- **Phone:** (518) 891-4050
- **Website:** www.apa.ny.gov
  If you're planning any activities that involve navigating

protected areas or camping in designated spots, the Adirondack Park Agency (APA) is your best resource. They oversee much of what happens in this massive region and can guide you on park rules or regulations.

General Emergency Numbers

- **911**: This is the number to call for life-threatening emergencies or immediate assistance anywhere in the Adirondacks. Even if you're in a remote area, dial it first. If there's no signal, move to higher ground or open spaces to try again.
- **Non-Emergency Police Assistance:** New York State Police – **(518) 563-3761**
  For situations that don't require immediate attention (e.g., reporting suspicious activity or seeking directions to the nearest ranger station).

Forest Rangers: The Unsung Heroes

- **Forest Ranger Dispatch (24/7):** (518) 891-0235
  Forest rangers are the lifeline of the Adirondack wilderness. They're trained for search and rescue operations, fire response, and emergency medical assistance. I've encountered them during a rescue mission after a hiker twisted their ankle deep in the High Peaks Wilderness—they were nothing short of incredible. If you're lost, injured, or stuck in an unsafe area, these are the people to call.

Hospitals and Medical Care

Should you or someone in your group need immediate medical attention, knowing the closest hospitals can save valuable time. Here are a few major options within the Adirondacks:

- **Adirondack Medical Center – Saranac Lake**
  Phone: (518) 891-4141
  Address: 2233 State Route 86, Saranac Lake, NY 12983
  This hospital is well-equipped and close to many popular destinations, including the High Peaks area. I once visited their ER after a nasty fall on icy trails near Mount Marcy—they're efficient and compassionate.
- **Glens Falls Hospital**
  Phone: (518) 926-1000
  Address: 100 Park St, Glens Falls, NY 12801
  Located in the southern part of the Adirondacks, this hospital is easily accessible if you're exploring Lake George or its surrounding trails.
- **Champlain Valley Physicians Hospital (CVPH)**
  Phone: (518) 561-2000
  Address: 75 Beekman St, Plattsburgh, NY 12901
  A reliable choice if you're in the northern regions, such as the Lake Champlain or Ausable Chasm areas.

Poison Control

- **New York Poison Control Center:** (800) 222-1222
  Whether it's an accidental ingestion of wild berries or a misstep with camping stove fuel, the Poison Control Center provides expert advice on managing potential poisoning situations. I remember calling them once when a friend mistakenly ate a wild plant he thought

was edible (it wasn't). They were calm, thorough, and helped us avoid a trip to the ER.

Fire Departments and Rescue Squads

The Adirondacks are dotted with small-town fire departments and rescue squads, many of which are volunteer-run. These teams are well-versed in local terrain and are often the first responders in emergencies.

- **Lake Placid Fire Department**: (518) 523-3211
  Serving the bustling Lake Placid area, this department is especially responsive during peak tourist seasons.
- **Tupper Lake Volunteer Fire Department**: (518) 359-9344
  Covering Tupper Lake and nearby regions, they're great for emergencies in this serene part of the park.

Animal Encounters and Wildlife Emergencies

It's not uncommon to come across wildlife while exploring the Adirondacks. If you encounter a bear, moose, or other potentially dangerous animal, you can contact the **New York Department of Environmental Conservation (DEC) Wildlife Unit** for guidance:

- **DEC Region 5 Office:** (518) 897-1200

Once, I was startled by a black bear while hiking. Thankfully, I had read up on bear behavior and carried bear spray, but it's comforting to know help is available if things escalate.

Roadside Assistance

Navigating Adirondack roads, especially in winter, can be challenging. Whether it's a flat tire or a car stuck in snow, roadside assistance is a must-have:

- **AAA Roadside Assistance:** (800) 222-4357
- **New York State Thruway Emergency Assistance:** (800) 842-2233

During one particularly icy winter trip, my car slid into a ditch on a backroad near Old Forge. AAA was a lifesaver, sending a tow truck to get me back on track.

Local Utility Emergencies

Power outages or downed trees blocking access are not uncommon in rural Adirondack towns, especially during storms. For utility emergencies:

- **National Grid (Electric and Gas):** (800) 867-5222
- **New York State Electric & Gas (NYSEG):** (800) 572-1131

Visitor Centers for Non-Emergency Help

Visitor centers across the Adirondacks are great for general inquiries or minor assistance. They often have maps, Wi-Fi access, and knowledgeable staff.

- **Adirondack Welcome Center**: (518) 668-5717
  Address: I-87 Northbound, Queensbury, NY 12804
  A perfect stop if you're entering the park from the south.

- **Paul Smith's College VIC (Visitor Interpretive Center)**: (518) 327-6241
  Located near Saranac Lake, this center offers trails and expert advice on navigating the local terrain.

Tips for Staying Connected in Emergencies

1. **Invest in a Satellite Phone or GPS Device:** Cell reception is unreliable in many parts of the Adirondacks. I carry a Garmin inReach device—it's pricey but invaluable for sending SOS messages from remote areas.
2. **Download Offline Maps:** Apps like Gaia GPS or AllTrails Pro let you navigate without a cell signal.
3. **Carry a First Aid Kit:** It's a no-brainer, but you'd be surprised how often people overlook this. Add extras like blister pads and emergency blankets.

Getting Around the Adirondacks

Exploring the Adirondack region is an adventure in itself, and getting around adds to the charm of the experience. Nestled in upstate New York, this area is a blend of stunning wilderness, quaint towns, and hidden gems. Transportation options here are diverse but cater mainly to those who enjoy the great outdoors or have a flexible travel mindset. Having spent time navigating its winding roads and exploring its serene landscapes, let me share how you can best get around the Adirondacks.

By Car: The Ultimate Way to Explore

When it comes to getting around the Adirondacks, driving is king. The region's sprawling terrain and the sheer distance between towns make having a car the most practical choice. If you don't already have one, renting a car is highly recommended. Most rental agencies can be found in Albany or nearby cities like Saratoga Springs or Plattsburgh, which are common entry points to the Adirondacks.

Routes:
The Adirondacks are connected by a network of scenic highways and local roads. One of my favorites is **Route 73**, which takes you from the Northway (I-87) into Lake Placid, passing waterfalls and mountains along the way. The **Adirondack Northway (I-87)** is the major highway through the eastern edge of the park, making it a vital artery for travelers. Other iconic routes include the **Olympic Byway**, which loops through Lake Placid and Saranac Lake, and the **Central Adirondack Trail**, a picturesque drive through Old Forge and Blue Mountain Lake.

Fare:
Since this is self-driven, your costs are primarily fuel, which, depending on the season and your vehicle type, can range between $3.50–$4.50 per gallon.

Operating Hours:
Essentially, your car's hours are your own! Just keep an eye on gas stations—some in remote areas close early, so don't wait until the last minute to refuel.

Tips:
Driving through the Adirondacks is a treat, especially during fall when the leaves turn fiery hues. However, keep in mind that

cellular service can be spotty in some areas, so downloading maps or carrying a GPS device is a lifesaver.

Public Bus Services: A Budget-Friendly Option

While cars are the most convenient way, the Adirondacks aren't entirely inaccessible to those without them. Public buses do operate in the region, although the services are limited.

Mode of Transportation:
The **Adirondack Trailways** is the primary long-distance bus service connecting New York City and Albany to key Adirondack towns like Lake Placid, Saranac Lake, and Ticonderoga. Within towns, you might find local shuttle services, especially in popular areas like Lake Placid.

Routes:
Adirondack Trailways buses typically stop in major hubs along the way. For example, a route from Albany to Lake Placid might pass through Keene Valley and Saranac Lake. Once you arrive in town, the Lake Placid XPRSS shuttle is a great way to get around locally.

Fare:
Expect to pay anywhere between $20–$60 for a one-way Trailways ticket, depending on the distance. Local shuttle rides are often free or cost a few dollars per trip.

Operating Hours:
Trailways buses usually have a couple of departures per day, with schedules posted online. Local shuttles like the Lake Placid XPRSS operate from early morning (around 8 AM) to evening (6 PM or later), depending on the season.

Card/Token System:
Trailways accepts online ticket purchases or payments at the station. Local shuttles are often cash-based, so carrying small bills is handy.

Tips:
If you're using public buses, plan your day carefully, as schedules are limited and infrequent. Arriving early at stops ensures you don't miss your ride.

Railroads: A Scenic Journey

Trains might not be the fastest way to get around, but they're definitely one of the most memorable. The Adirondack Railroad, for example, is a nostalgic ride through some of the region's most picturesque areas.

Mode of Transportation:
The **Adirondack Railroad** offers scenic train rides rather than point-to-point transport. It's ideal for those who want to enjoy the journey as much as the destination.

Routes:
The Adirondack Railroad primarily runs between Utica and Old Forge, with stops at towns like Thendara. Seasonal routes, like the fall foliage tours, are incredibly popular and showcase the region's vibrant beauty.

Fare:
Tickets for a scenic ride range from $15–$50, depending on the route and the type of seat you choose.

Operating Hours:
Trains operate seasonally, with most services running from May

to October. Schedules vary, so it's best to check their website before planning your trip.

Tips:
Book tickets in advance, especially during peak seasons like summer and fall. Bring snacks and drinks, as some rides can be several hours long with limited food options.

Biking: For the Adventurous

For those who enjoy an active lifestyle, biking is a fantastic way to explore the Adirondacks. Whether you're cycling between towns or hitting the trails, this mode of transport lets you soak in the natural beauty at your own pace.

Routes:
Some of the best biking routes include the **Adirondack Coast Bikeways**, a collection of trails near Lake Champlain, and the **Warren County Bikeway**, which stretches from Lake George to Glens Falls. Mountain biking enthusiasts should check out trails in Wilmington or the extensive network at Gore Mountain.

Fare:
If you're renting a bike, expect costs of $30–$50 per day. If you bring your own, the cost is virtually zero!

Operating Hours:
Biking is a daylight activity, so plan your rides between sunrise and sunset for safety.

Tips:
Always carry water, a repair kit, and a map. Wearing bright clothing and a helmet is essential, especially on shared roads.

Taxis and Rideshares: Limited but Available

In towns like Lake Placid or Saranac Lake, you'll find local taxi services. Ridesharing apps like Uber and Lyft are available but can be spotty depending on the area and time of day.

Mode of Transportation:
Local taxis and occasional rideshare options.

Routes:
Taxis typically operate within towns or to nearby destinations. For example, a ride from Lake Placid to Saranac Lake is a common request.

Fare:
Taxi rides within towns range from $10–$30. Longer rides, such as airport transfers, may cost $50–$100.

Operating Hours:
Taxis are usually available from morning to late evening. Pre-booking is recommended, especially at night or in the off-season.

Tips:
Always confirm the fare before starting your ride. Tipping drivers (10–20%) is customary.

Water Transport: Unique to the Adirondacks

Given the abundance of lakes and waterways, ferries and water taxis are an iconic way to get around in certain areas.

Mode of Transportation:
Seasonal ferries and private water taxis.

Routes:
The **Lake Champlain Ferry** connects the Adirondacks with Vermont, offering scenic crossings. In other areas, water taxis operate on popular lakes like Lake George or Blue Mountain Lake.

Fare:
Ferry rides are affordable, typically $5–$15 per person. Private water taxis may charge $20–$50, depending on the distance.

Operating Hours:
Most water transport services operate from late spring to early fall, usually from 8 AM to sunset.

Tips:
If you're exploring by kayak or canoe, many lakes have launch sites. Renting a kayak costs around $20–$40 for a few hours.

Hiking: The Simplest Mode of Transport

Sometimes, the best way to get around the Adirondacks is on foot. With over 2,000 miles of hiking trails, this region is a hiker's paradise.

Routes:
Trails like the **High Peaks Wilderness** or the **Cascade Mountain Trail** are iconic. For a leisurely walk, consider the **Mirror Lake Loop** in Lake Placid.

Fare:
Hiking is free! Some trailheads require parking fees, usually around $5–$10.

Operating Hours:
Trails are open year-round, but hiking during daylight hours is safest.

Tips:
Dress in layers, carry plenty of water, and let someone know your route before heading out.

Made in the USA
Monee, IL
30 May 2025